The Least You Should Know About Vocabulary Building

Word Roots

Eighth Edition

Carol E. Friend
Mercer County Community College

Laura D. Knight
Mercer County Community College

Teresa Ferster Glazier
Late, Western Illinois University

CENGAGE
Learning·

Australia • Brazil • Mexico • Singapore • United Kingdom • United States

CENGAGE
Learning®

The Least You Should Know about Vocabulary Building: Word Roots, Eighth Edition
Carol E. Friend,
Laura D. Knight,
Teresa Ferster Glazier, Late

Product Director: Annie Todd

Senior Product Manager: Shani Fisher

Senior Content Developer: Kathy Sands-Boehmer

Content Coordinator: Erin Nixon

Product Assistant: Erin Nixon

Media Developer: Amy Gibbons

Marketing Manager: Lydia Lestar

Rights Acquisitions Specialist: Ann Hoffman

Manufacturing Planner: Betsy Donaghey

Art and Design Direction, Production Management, and Composition: Cenveo® Publisher Services

Cover Image: © Gettyimages.com

For product information and technology assistance, contact us at **Cengage Learning Customer & Sales Support, 1-800-354-9706**

For permission to use material from this text or product, submit all requests online at **www.cengage.com/permissions**. Further permissions questions can be emailed to **permissionrequest@cengage.com**.

Library of Congress Control Number: 2013948729

ISBN-13: 978-1-285-43045-4

ISBN-10: 1-285-43045-X

Cengage Learning
200 First Stamford Place, 4th Floor
Stamford, CT 06902
USA

Cengage Learning is a leading provider of customized learning solutions with office locations around the globe, including Singapore, the United Kingdom, Australia, Mexico, Brazil, and Japan. Locate your local office at **international.cengage.com/region**.

Cengage Learning products are represented in Canada by Nelson Education, Ltd.

For your course and learning solutions, visit **www.cengage.com**.

Purchase any of our products at your local college store or at our preferred online store **www.cengagebrain.com**.

Instructors: Please visit **login.cengage.com** and log in to access instructor-specific resources.

Printed in the United States of America
1 2 3 4 5 6 7 17 16 15 14 13

Contents

To the Instructor

Because learning to break words into their parts is perhaps the most important initial step in vocabulary building, this text helps students take that step and begin what should become an ongoing study of words. Whether the text is used in the classroom or for self-help, the following features make it easy to use with little guidance.

1. Because only one approach is used—word roots—students can work through the text easily. They learn a method of study while learning the first root and follow it throughout the book.

2. No distinction is made between Greek and Latin roots. Students need to remember the meaning of a root rather than its language source. Similarly, no distinction is made among roots, prefixes, and suffixes because all are equally sources of word meaning.

3. Students learn words in context. After a word is defined, it is then used in a sentence.

4. Difficult words are included for those who happen to be ready for them, but students should be encouraged to concentrate on words they have encountered before and are curious about.

5. The simplest pronunciation aids are used: the only diacritical marks being the one for long vowels and accent marks for syllable stress.

6. Part of speech is provided to help students understand how the word is used in the example sentence.

7. A Word Index is included to help students find words in the text.

8. A Student Companion website, located at www.cengagebrain.com, offers students the answer key for textbook exercises as well as audio flashcards.

9. The Instructor Companion website, located at www.cengagebrain.com, includes the Test Bank for use with this text.

New to the Eighth Edition

In this revision for *The Least You Should Know about Vocabulary Building: Word Roots*, we added the root—RUPT, updated many of the exercises, and created new sections throughout the text called EXTRA PRACTICE. Also, answers to all exercises and online audio flashcards have been added to the website. We continue to maintain the original format because it is successful as it stands.

Acknowledgments

Thanks to our editor, Kathy Sands-Boehmer and also to our reviewers for this edition who offered comments and suggestions: Mary Carstens, Wayne State University; Pamela Krueger, Bismarck State College; Terri LaRocco, University of Findlay; Ann-Marie Obilade, Alcorn State University; Daniela Rodriguez, Texas A&M International University; and Sheri Van Court, Brookhaven College, and to our loyal users for their continued support.

A special note of thanks to our families.

—Carol E. Friend and Laura D. Knight

Increasing Your Vocabulary Through Learning Word Roots

How did words get to be words? Why, for example, is a hippopotamus called a hippopotamus and not a glipserticka? There's a good reason. Because the animal looks a bit like a fat horse and spends much of its time in rivers, the Greeks combined their word for horse, HIPPOS, and their word for river, POTAMOS, and called the animal a hippopotamos, a river horse. And with only a one-letter change, the word has come down to us as hippopotamus.

Words did not just happen. They grew. And if you learn how they grew—what original roots[1] they came from—you'll find it easier to remember them. You'll *understand* the words you look up in the dictionary instead of just memorizing the definitions. And weeks later, even though you may have forgotten the meaning of a word, your knowledge of its roots will help you recall its meaning.

The best first step in vocabulary building, then, is to become familiar with some word roots because learning the root of one word often gives a clue to dozens or hundreds more. For example, if you learn that SYN (SYM, SYL) means *together* or *with*, you have a clue to more than 450 words, for that many words begin with SYN (SYM, SYL). Similarly, when you learn that *philanthropist* is made up of PHIL *to love* and ANTHROP *human*, you have learned not only that a philanthropist is a lover of humanity, but you also have a clue to some 70 other words beginning with PHIL and to more than 60 others beginning with ANTHROP, not to mention those that have PHIL or ANTHROP in the middle or at the end of the word.

As you become aware of how words are made up, familiar words will take on new meaning, and unfamiliar words may often be understood even without a dictionary. For instance, if you know that the root BIBL means *book* as in *bibliography* and *Bible*, then you can guess that a *bibliophile* will have something to do with books. And if you remember that PHIL means *to love*, as in *philanthropist* (lover of humanity), then you will immediately guess that a bibliophile must be a lover of books.

Glancing at the root chain following this paragraph will help you spot some common roots. The chain begins with *biped* [BI two + PED foot], a two-footed animal. The next word contains one of the preceding roots, PED. A *pedometer* [PED foot + METER measure] is, as its roots indicate, "a foot measure" or an instrument that measures the distance walked by recording the number of steps taken. The next word must contain METER, and out of the hundreds of METER words, *geometry* [GEO earth + METER measure] has been chosen. As its roots show, geometry was originally a system of "Earth measuring," that is, of measuring the Earth through the use of angles. The next word must contain GEO, and so on.

---

[1] In this book, the term *roots* includes prefixes and suffixes because all word parts are equally sources of word meaning. All are the roots from which our language comes.

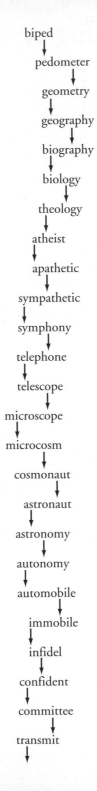

transport
↓
report
↓
recur
↓
excursion
↓
exclude
↓
seclude
↓
secure
↓
manicure
↓
manuscript
↓
subscribe
↓
subversive
↓
controversy
↓
contradict
↓
benediction
↓
benefactor
↓
facilitate

This root chain ends with *facilitate* (to make easier). Perhaps reading the chain will facilitate your spotting word roots in the future.

After you've learned some of the roots in this book, try to make a root chain of your own.

Learning word roots is not only the quickest way to increase your vocabulary but also the most entertaining. For example, did you know . . .

that **salary** [SAL salt] originally was the money paid to Roman soldiers to buy salt . . .

that a **companion** [COM with + PAN bread] was originally a person one shared one's bread with . . .

that **malaria** [MAL bad + AER air] was so named because people thought it was caused by the bad air of the swamps . . .

that a **terrier** [TERR earth] got its name because it digs in the earth after small animals in burrows . . .

that **escape** [ES out + CAP cape] originally meant to get out of one's cape, leaving it in the hands of the pursuer . . .

that an **insect** [IN in + SECT to cut] was so named because its body is "cut" into three segments . . .

that a **bonfire** in the Middle Ages was the bone fire built to dispose of corpses during the plague . . .

that **panic** originally described the frantic efforts of the Greek nymphs to escape when the mischievous god Pan suddenly appeared among them . . .

that **curfew** in the Middle Ages in France was the ringing of a bell telling the peasants to cover their fires (*couvre-feu*) for the night . . .

that **alphabet** comes from the first two letters of the Greek alphabet, ALPHA and BETA, "a" and "b" . . .

that **trivia** [TRI three + VIA way] in Roman times meant the crossroads where three ways met and where neighborhood gossips on their way to market often stopped to chat about unimportant things (TRI VIA talk) . . .

that **preposterous** [PRE before + POST after] originally meant having the before part where the after part should be, like a horse with its tail where its head should be—in other words, absurd.

As you look up words in the dictionary, you may uncover other interesting stories if you note the word roots, which will usually be found after the definition.

Changes in Root Spelling

A root may change its spelling slightly according to the word it is in. For example, EX *out* is found in **excursion**, but it changes to ES in **escape** and to simply E in **educate**. Such changes have occurred to make pronunciation easier. Escape and educate are easier to pronounce than excape and exducate would be. Here are some of the ways root spellings change.

Sometimes the last letter of a root changes to be like the first letter of the root that follows:

COM nect	becomes	CON nect
COM loquial	becomes	COL loquial
COM relate	becomes	COR relate
DIS fident	becomes	DIF fident
SYN metrical	becomes	SYM metrical

Sometimes the last letter of a root changes (or is dropped) to make the pronunciation easier, but it doesn't become the same as the first letter of the root that follows:

EX cape	becomes	ES cape
COM temporary	becomes	CON temporary
SYN pathy	becomes	SYM pathy
DIS vert	becomes	DI vert
EX ducate	becomes	E ducate

A root may also appear in slightly different forms in different words. CLUD, *to close, to shut,* may appear as

CLUD	in	seclude
CLUS	in	recluse
CLAUS	in	claustrophobia
CLOS	in	closet

but you'll soon learn to spot a root even when its spelling varies.

How to Use This Book

It makes little difference which root you study first because each root will eventually help you with some new word. Therefore, the roots in this text are presented alphabetically.

As you work through the book, you may come across words with which you are unfamiliar. This is to be expected and will make studying this book challenging and rewarding. Working with word roots and the words that are formed from the roots will make your learning easier. After you learn the roots, you will notice that you can figure out the meaning of other words. Mastering even a few words under each root will boost your vocabulary.

Here is how to begin your study:

1. First, take the PRELIMINARY TEST on page 8. At the end of your study, you will have a chance to take COMPREHENSIVE TESTS to see how the study of word roots has increased your vocabulary.

2. Now turn to the first root—A, AN on page 12. The root and its meaning are provided, followed by a short story showing the origin of the root.

   Each word is identified in **bold**, followed by its (pronunciation in parentheses), followed by [root meaning in square brackets], and followed by its part of speech—noun, verb, adjective, or adverb.

   For help with pronunciation see the **Pronunciation Key** on the inside front cover of this book.

   (Note that not every root of every word is explained but only those that will help you remember the word.)

   The first definition may be a literal one (marked "literally") taken directly from the meaning of the roots. The definitions that follow are current. Following the definition is a sentence in *italics* that shows its meaning in context.

3. After you have studied all the words on the page, do the exercises that follow and check your answers online at www.cengagebrain.com.

4. Once you complete the exercises provided, you can further your study with word lists, journal entries, and word chains. Flashcards for additional practice are available at www.cengagebrain.com.

5. In addition, after every five roots that you have studied, you will have an opportunity to test yourself in the EXTRA PRACTICE sections.

6. As you progress through the book, the words may become more challenging, but you should begin to notice how each word root is used in multiple ways.

   A good way to remember new words is to use some of the words in your own writing. *Putting the words into your own writing will help you remember them longer than if you merely fill in blanks.* From time to time, reread your journal to review your words.

7. Finally, take the most important step in vocabulary building—use your newly learned words in conversation. *Using a word in conversation will do more to help you remember it than any amount of silent study. Use a word three times and it's yours.* Try using one new word a day. Begin at breakfast, and during the day find two more opportunities to use the word. After you have used it three times, you'll be surprised how easily it will slip into your conversation. Even if it's a word you don't expect to use, it will stay in your passive vocabulary so that you'll recognize it when you encounter it in your reading.

PRELIMINARY TEST

Test yourself on these words taken from college textbooks and current magazines. Check your answers in the online Answer Key.

1. _____ **ambiguous**   **A.** very large   **B.** having two possible meanings   **C.** seeking fame   **D.** exceptionally clear

2. _____ **philanthropic**   **A.** criticism   **B.** fond of animals   **C.** sociable   **D.** charitable

3. _____ **antipathy**   **A.** strong dislike   **B.** worry   **C.** kind   **D.** ancient

4. _____ **autonomous**   **A.** self-governing   **B.** governed by a few   **C.** governed by a dictator   **D.** without any government

5. _____ **benefactor**   **A.** one who receives money from a will   **B.** one who receives a grant   **C.** distant relative   **D.** one who gives assistance

6. _____ **anachronism**   **A.** mistake in grammar   **B.** something out of its proper historical time   **C.** incorrect calculation   **D.** clock for navigation

7. _____ **circumscribe**   **A.** to overcome circumstances   **B.** to write an autograph   **C.** to restrict the action of   **D.** to denounce

8. _____ **convivial**   **A.** sociable   **B.** superficial   **C.** dangerous to life   **D.** vivid

9. _____ **credulous**   **A.** unbelieving   **B.** believing too readily   **C.** suspicious   **D.** happy

10. _____ **precursor**   **A.** supervisor   **B.** beginner   **C.** forerunner   **D.** financial officer

11. _____ **pandemic**   **A.** causing illness   **B.** a wild uproar   **C.** democratic   **D.** widespread

12. _____ **euphemism**   **A.** substitution of a pleasant for an unpleasant word   **B.** substitution of a specific term for a general one   **C.** false statement   **D.** unrestrained praise

13. _____ **enervate**   **A.** to weaken   **B.** to strengthen   **C.** to soothe   **D.** to excite

14. _____ **epilogue**   **A.** a funeral   **B.** speech at the end of a play   **C.** tragedy   **D.** apology

15. _____ **loquacious**   **A.** full of life   **B.** having the ability to see things clearly   **C.** understanding several languages   **D.** talkative

16. _____ **malinger**   **A.** move slowly   **B.** spend too much time on details   **C.** pretend to be ill to get out of work   **D.** waste time

17. _____ **amoral**   **A.** lost article   **B.** missing part   **C.** wrong answer   **D.** neither moral or immoral

18. _____ **metamorphosis**   **A.** life of a butterfly   **B.** change of form   **C.** mental illness   **D.** abnormal growth

19. _____ **panacea**   **A.** remedy for all ills   **B.** folktale   **C.** widespread   **D.** mountaintop

20. _____ **apathy**   **A.** dislike   **B.** strong interest   **C.** indifference   **D.** sympathy

21. _____ **impediment**   **A.** lack of funds   **B.** hindrance   **C.** language   **D.** a tool

22. _____ **progeny**   **A.** plan of action   **B.** gifted child   **C.** descendants   **D.** ancestors

23. _____ **assiduous**   **A.** overbearing   **B.** haughty   **C.** critical   **D.** persevering

24. _____ **auspicious**   **A.** unfavorable   **B.** favorable   **C.** evil   **D.** quiet

25. _____ **subterranean**   **A.** a covering   **B.** suburb   **C.** under the earth   **D.** unlikely

26. _____ **supercilious**   **A.** haughty   **B.** socially prominent   **C.** intellectually superior
    D. solicitous

27. _____ **syndrome**   **A.** place where horse races are held   **B.** stadium   **C.** two adjoining
    domes   **D.** symptoms occurring together

28. _____ **profuse**   **A.** angry   **B.** happy   **C.** generous   **D.** sad

29. _____ **tortuous**   **A.** a large turtle   **B.** full of twists and turns   **C.** severe mental or
    physical pain   **D.** large and foreboding

30. _____ **vocation**   **A.** time off   **B.** pastime   **C.** territory   **D.** profession

31. _____ **avert**   **A.** to pay attention to   **B.** to turn toward   **C.** to turn away from   **D.** an
    advertisement

32. _____ **veracious**   **A.** honest   **B.** inaccurate   **C.** unhappy   **D.** fanciful

33. _____ **anniversary**   **A.** twisted   **B.** two-prong spear   **C.** annual return of event
    D. a three-legged camera support

34. _____ **antecedent**   **A.** strong feeling of dislike   **B.** ancient times   **C.** occur before
    something else   **D.** word, phrase, or clause to which a pronoun refers

35. _____ **bicuspid**   **A.** a tooth having two points   **B.** a celebration   **C.** two marriages
    D. both branches of government

36. _____ **recur**   **A.** to race   **B.** to receive   **C.** to send   **D.** to happen again

37. _____ **infidelity**   **A.** unfaithfulness   **B.** unhappiness   **C.** bonus check   **D.** spirited

38. _____ **symphony**   **A.** talk against   **B.** orchestra   **C.** religious service   **D.** showing
    concern

39. _____ **posterior**   **A.** upright part of fence   **B.** calling out   **C.** unusually large
    D. located behind

40. _____ **pertain**   **A.** to belong   **B.** to exclude   **C.** to sail   **D.** to humor

WORD ROOTS IN ALPHABETICAL ORDER

1   A, AN—not, without; unusual or irregular

When A or AN comes at the beginning of certain words, it gives those words a meaning of *not* or *without*. Anything that is **asymmetrical** is *not* symmetrical, and anything that is **atypical** is *not* typical, meaning *unusual* or *irregular*.

Atheist and **agnostic** both begin with A and are close in meaning. An atheist [A without + THE god] is *without* a God, whereas an agnostic [A not + GNOS to know] does *not* know whether there is a God. In other words, the atheist is sure there is no God, whereas the agnostic simply does not know.

agnostic (ag nos´ tik) [A not + GNOS to know] noun—one who does not know whether there is a God. *He had lost his former faith and had become an agnostic.*

amoral (ā mawr´ ul) adjective—unable to distinguish between right and wrong; neither moral nor immoral. *Infants are amoral because they have not learned the difference between right and wrong.*

anarchy (an´ ur ke) [AN without + ARCH ruler or leader] noun—literally without a ruler; political disorder and confusion. *The overthrow of the government resulted in anarchy.*

anecdote (an´ ik dōt) [AN not + EKDOTOS given out] noun—a short account of an interesting or humorous incident that is an aside to the main idea. *The speaker began his talk with an entertaining anecdote.*

anemia (un ne´ me uh) [AN without + HEM blood] noun—a deficiency of red blood cells. *Her weakness was caused by anemia.*

anesthesia (an is the´ zeh) [AN without + ESTHET feeling] noun—a drug that causes one to be insensitive to pain. *Before the operation, he was given anesthesia.*

anomaly (uh nom´ uh lē) [AN not + HOMO same] noun—a rare exception; something that is not normal. An example of an anomaly in nature is the ostrich, a bird that cannot fly.

anonymous (uh non´ uh mus) [AN without + ONYM name] adjective—having an unknown or unacknowledged name. *The donor of the new hospital wing wished to remain anonymous.*

asymmetrical (ā si met´ ri kul) adjective—not having both sides exactly alike; not symmetrical. *At the fashion show, some designers featured asymmetrical hemlines.*

atheist (ā the ist) [A without + THE god] noun—one who is without a God; one who denies the existence of God. *As an atheist, she objected to the nativity scene in the town square at Christmas.*

atypical (ā tip´ i kul) adjective—not typical. *A classical concert performed by a rock band would certainly be atypical.*

ALSO: amorphous, analgesic, apathetic, apathy. (Some of these words are discussed under their other roots in the Word Index on page 165.)

✎ **EXERCISE 1**   Write the A, AN word next to its definition.

1. _____ political disorder
2. _____ one who does not know if there is a God
3. _____ a rare exception
4. _____ not having both sides exactly alike
5. _____ unable to distinguish between right and wrong

✎ **EXERCISE 2**   Write the appropriate A, AN word.

1. To add interest, the professor sprinkled her lectures with _____.
2. Jolene cried when she saw her _____ haircut: one side was three inches longer than the other.
3. Most famous people like being recognized when it is convenient for them but prefer being _____ when it is not.
4. Bryn was late to class, which was _____ of her behavior.
5. _____ erupted when the protesters ran wild through the streets shouting slogans, breaking windows, and overturning cars.
6. After ten years, Jose quit the ministry and announced he was now an _____ because he no longer believed there was a God.
7. Sheila is _____ and questions whether or not there is a God.
8. Researchers used to think that animals were _____, but now some think that animals do follow a moral code.
9. The dentist gave _____ to the patient before pulling all her teeth.
10. To fight her _____, the doctor prescribed iron pills.
11. His outgoing nature made him an _____ in his shy family.

✎ **EXERCISE 3 JOURNAL**   In your *vocabulary journal*, write three to five sentences using some of the A, AN words you have studied. Be sure your sentences show each word's definition.

2 AMBI, AMPHI—around, both

In Roman times, candidates for public office, wearing white togas so that they could be easily seen, walked *around* (AMBI) talking to people and seeking votes. Before long, the term *ambitio* took on the meaning of bribery in seeking votes, but by the time the word came into English in the fourteenth century as **ambitious**, it had lost the idea of seeking votes or of bribery and meant merely "eager to succeed or to advance."

In the following words, AMBI or AMPHI means *around*:

ambience (am´ be uns) [AMBI around] noun—the surrounding atmosphere. *The bonsai plants and the paper dragons give the Japanese restaurant a pleasant ambience.*

ambitious (am bish´ us)) [AMBI around] adjective—having a desire to succeed. *She is ambitious, working hard to get a better job.*

amphitheater (am fuh the´ tur)) [AMBI around] noun—an oval or a round structure with tiers of seats around an open space. *The Drama Department presented* Twelve Angry Men *in the university's amphitheater.*

In the following words, AMBI or AMPHI means *both*:

ambidextrous (am bi dek´ strus) [AMBI both + DEXTR right hand] adjective—able to use both hands with equal ease. *Because she is ambidextrous, she plays a great game of tennis.*

ambiguity (am bi gyO´ uh te) [AMBI both] noun—the quality of having two possible meanings. *The ambiguity in his writing leaves the reader puzzled.*

ambiguous (am big´ yO us) [AMBI both + AGERE to drive] adjective—uncertain; having two possible meanings. *Jayne felt ambiguous about dating Henry.*

ambivalence (am biv´ uh luns) [AMBI both] noun—conflicting (both kinds of) feelings toward a person or thing. *The boy was experiencing ambivalence about giving his speech, wanting to give it and yet dreading it.*

ambivalent (am biv´ uh lunt) [AMBI both] adjective—having conflicting (both kinds of) feelings toward someone or something. *A child often feels ambivalent about a new baby in the family, both liking it and resenting it.*

amphibian (am fib´ e un) [AMPHI both + BIO life] noun—an animal that lives both in water and on land. *Frogs, toads, and salamanders are amphibians.* Also, an aircraft that can take off and land both on water and on land.

amphibious (am fib´ e us) [AMPHI both + BIO life] adjective—able to live or to travel both on land and in water. *The Marines went ashore in amphibious vehicles.*

ALSO: ambient, ambition, amphipathic

EXERCISE 1   Write the AMBI, AMPHI word next to its definition.

1. _____ having conflicting feelings toward a person or thing
2. _____ having two possible meanings
3. _____ able to use both hands with equal ease
4. _____ an open structure with tiers of seats around an open space
5. _____ having a desire to be successful
6. _____ an animal that lives both on land and in water
7. _____ the surrounding atmosphere
8. _____ able to live or to travel both on water and on land

EXERCISE 2   Write the appropriate AMBI, AMPHI word.

1. The _____ of the country lodge was warm and friendly.

2. The hovercraft is an _____ vehicle.

3. Ben didn't stop writing when he broke his right arm because he is _____.

4. Jenna's _____ about hosting the Garden Club's party was obvious; she was both excited and nervous.

5. Herpetologists study frogs and other _____.

6. The town built an _____ so the members of the drama club would have a place to perform their plays.

7. The witness' statement was filled with _____, so the police did not know whom to arrest.

8. Josh never misses a class and studies several hours each day; he is very _____.

9. His _____ answer left me wondering which door to open.

10. Being afraid of heights but loving adventure, she has _____ feelings about learning to fly a plane.

EXERCISE 3 JOURNAL   Write three sentences in your *vocabulary journal* about going to a theatrical performance using some of the AMBI, AMPHI words you have learned. Check with the sentence given in the explanation of each word to make sure you are using the word correctly. For example, *ambiguous* is an adjective, whereas *ambiguity* is a noun. But even without thinking about the parts of speech, you'll use the words correctly if you follow the model sentences.

3 ANN, ENN—year

Each **year** turns into the next with remembrances we note on their **anniversary**. Words containing ANN or ENN will have something to do with *year*. An **annuity** is a fund that pays a person money every *year*. **Annual** means happening every *year*, and **semiannual** means happening every half *year*. **Biannual** and **biennial** are easily confused because they both come from BI *two* and ANN or ENN *year*. Just remember that **biannual** and **semiannual** (both meaning twice a year) sound alike, whereas **biennial** (meaning every two years) sounds different.

annals (an′ uls) [ANN year] noun—a written account of events year by year; historical records. *We searched the annals of the medical society to find when the vaccine had first been tested.*

anniversary (an uh vurs′ uh re) [ANN year + VERS to turn] noun—the yearly return of the date of some memorable event. *We're making plans for our parents' wedding anniversary.*

annual (an′ yO ul) [ANN year] adjective—yearly. *We have an annual family reunion.* Also, lasting only one year, as an annual plant. *She liked annual plants even though she had to replace them every year.*

annuity (uh nO′ uh te) [ANN year] noun—an investment that provides fixed payments yearly or at other regular intervals. *After paying into his annuity for years, he now receives a check every month.*

biannual (bi an′ yOul) [BI two + ANN year] adjective—occurring two times a year. *The treasurer made biannual reports in January and July.*

biennial (bi en′ ē ul) [BI two + ENN year] adjective—occurring every two years. *The society holds a biennial convention in the odd-numbered years.*

centennial (sen ten′ ē ul) [CENT hundred + ENN year] noun—a hundredth anniversary. *The Exposition in Montreal in 1967 celebrated the centennial of Canadian Confederation.*

millennium (muh len′ ē um) [MILLI thousand + ENN year] noun—a period of a thousand years. *We celebrated the start of the new millennium in the year 2000.*

per annum (pur an′ um) [PER through + ANN year] noun—by the year; annually. *The chairperson received a fixed salary per annum.*

perennial (puh ren′ ē ul) [PER through + ENN year] noun—having a life cycle lasting through more than two years, as a perennial plant. *In his garden, he planted only perennials so that he wouldn't have to replant every year.* Also, lasting many years, as perennial youth. *She was a perennial student, still taking courses after she was 50.*

semiannual (sem ē an′ yO ul) [SEMI half + ANN year] adjective—half yearly; occurring two times a year. *He made semiannual reports in January and July.*

superannuated (sO pur an′ yO ā tid) [SUPER over + ANN year] adjective—retired because of age. *Although he was superannuated, he still felt useful and volunteered his talents.* Also antiquated or obsolete, out of date. *We should not be held back by superannuated beliefs.*

ALSO: *anno Domini* (abbreviated AD), bicentennial, triennial

EXERCISE 1 Write the correct ANN, ENN word next to its definition.

1. _____ yearly

2. _____ occurring two times a year

3. _____ hundredth anniversary

4. _____ retired because of age or out of date

5. _____ period of a thousand years

EXERCISE 2 Write the appropriate ANN, ENN word.

1. The bank report is due _____ every January and June.

2. The _____ celebration is held on every even-numbered year.

3. Koji's _____ pays him $500 a month.

4. The _____ of *Joseon Dynasty* are records of Korean history.

5. All employees in the company become _____ at the age of seventy.

6. The African daisy has bold leaves and large flowers, but as an _____ it has to be replanted each year.

7. The years 2001 to 3000 are the current _____.

8. The magazine subscription costs $25 _____.

9. The clothing store has its _____ sale every spring and fall.

10. I love _____ flowers because I don't have to replant them each year.

11. The owners of the shop celebrated their first _____ with a sale to thank their customers.

12. As part of the town's _____ celebration, the Park Department planted one hundred trees.

EXERCISE 3 JOURNAL Write three sentences in your *vocabulary journal* about banking and business using many of the ANN, ENN words you have learned. Check the sentence given in the explanation of each word to make sure you are using the word correctly.

4 ANTE, ANTI—before

The ANTE spelling always means *before*—either *before* in place or *before* in time. **Anteroom** and **anterior** are *before* in place, whereas **ante** and **antedate** are *before* in time.

ante (an´ te) [ANTE before] noun—the amount each poker player must put into the pot before receiving his cards. *Feeling confident, he upped the ante.*

antecedent (an tuh sēd´ unt) [ANTE before + CED to go] noun—anything that logically goes before something else. *Cricket is the antecedent of baseball.* Also, the word, phrase, or clause to which a pronoun refers. *In the sentence "Every boy was in his place," boy is the antecedent of the pronoun his.*

antedate (an´ ti date) [ANTE before] verb—to occur before something else. *The Revolutionary War antedates the Civil War.*

ante meridiem (an ti muh rid´ ē um) (abbreviated AM) [ANTE before + MERIDI noon + DIEM day] noun—before noon. *I have an appointment at 10 AM.*

anterior (an tir´ ē ur) [ANTE before] adjective—located before or in front. *The anterior legs of the kangaroo are shorter than the posterior ones.*

anteroom (an´ ti rOm) [ANTE before] noun—a room before the main room; a waiting room. *In the director's anteroom were a dozen actors waiting to try out for the part.*

A variant spelling—ANTI—also means *before* in time in the following words.

anticipate (an tis´ uh pāt) [ANTI before + CIPARE to take care of] verb—to realize beforehand. *No one anticipated such an outcome.*

antiquated (an´ tuh kwa tid) [ANTI before] adjective—so old as to be no longer useful. *The factory had to replace the antiquated machinery.*

antique (an tek´) [ANTI before] noun—belonging to an earlier (before) period. *In the parade were a dozen antique automobiles.*

antiquity (an tik´ wuh tē) [ANTI before] noun—ancient (before) times. *The museum specializes in armor from antiquity.*

(ANTI meaning *against* or *opposite* will be found on page 24.)

✎ **EXERCISE 1**   **Match each word to its definition.**

1. _____ antiquity   **A.** a room before the main room; a waiting room

2. _____ antecedent   **B.** to realize beforehand

3. _____ anteroom   **C.** ancient (before) times

4. _____ anticipate   **D.** anything that logically goes before something

✎ **EXERCISE 2**   **Write the appropriate ANTE, ANTI word.**

1. In the sentence "The actors knew their lines," the word "their" is the _____ of "actors."

2. The doctor's _____ was filled with waiting patients.

3. The _____ oak desk sold for $1,000 at the auction.

4. No one _____ (s) a traffic jam at 4 A.M.

5. Before the cards were dealt, all the players placed their _____ on the table.

6. The taxidermist learned that the head is the _____ and the rump is the posterior.

7. The _____ computer cannot run any of the new programs I need for school.

8. Radio _____ television.

9. The history professor studied the pottery shards from _____.

10. As an early riser, I enjoy the _____.

✎ **EXERCISE 3 JOURNAL**   **Write three sentences in your *vocabulary journal* about a visit to a museum using some of the ANTE, ANTI words you have learned. Check with the sentences given in the explanation of each word to make sure you are using the word correctly.**

5 ANTHROP—human

Knowing that ANTHROP means *human* clarifies the meaning of a number of words. **Anthropology** [ANTHROP human + -LOGY study of] is a study of the development and behavior of *human* beings. A **philanthropist** [PHIL to love + ANTHROP human] loves *human* beings and promotes *human* welfare by charitable acts or gifts. A **misanthrope** [MIS to hate + ANTHROP human], on the other hand, hates *human* beings.

anthropoid (an´ thruh poid) [ANTHROP human + OID resembling] noun—resembling humans. *Gorillas, chimpanzees, orangutans, and gibbons are anthropoid apes.*

anthropologist (an thruh pol´ uh jist) [ANTHROP human + -LOGY study of] noun—one who studies the physical, social, and cultural development and behavior of human beings. *The anthropologist Margaret Mead lived for a time in Samoa studying the Samoan culture.*

anthropology (an thruh pol´ uh je) [ANTHROP human + -LOGY study of] noun—a study of the physical, social, and cultural development and behavior of human beings. *Applied anthropology is used to solve modern social problems.*

anthropomorphic (an thruh po mawr´ fik) [ANTHROP human + MORPH form] adjective—a god, animal, or inanimate thing thought of as having human form or characteristics. *The animal characters in Beatrix Potter's* Peter Rabbit *are anthropomorphic.*

anthropomorphism (an thruh po mawr´ fiz um) [ANTHROP human + MORPH form] noun—attributing human form or characteristics to a god, animal, or inanimate thing. *Anthropomorphism is a part of many primitive cultures, with rivers, trees, and animals being given human characteristics.*

misanthrope (mis´ un thrōp) [MIS to hate + ANTHROP human] noun—one who hates people. *Only a misanthrope would have such a low opinion of the human race.*

misanthropic (mis un throp´ ik) [MIS to hate + ANTHROP human] adjective—characterized by hatred or scorn for people. *Ebenezer Scrooge shows his misanthropic attitude when he replies to a Christmas greeting with "Bah! Humbug!"*

philanthropic (fil un throp´ ik) [PHIL to love + ANTHROP human] adjective—charitable. *The United Fund supports many philanthropic organizations.*

philanthropist (fi lan´ thruh pist) [PHIL to love + ANTHROP human] noun—one who loves people, particularly one who gives money to benefit humanity. *Andrew Carnegie, a famous philanthropist, gave money to build public libraries.*

philanthropy (fil lan´ thruh pē) [PHIL to love + ANTHROP human] noun—the effort to increase the well-being of humanity by charitable donations. *The corporation was known for its philanthropy as well as for its good business practices.*

EXERCISE 1   Write the ANTHROP word next to its definition.

1. _____ the attributing of human form or characteristics to a god, animal, or inanimate thing

2. _____ one who hates people _____ one who loves people, particularly one who gives money to benefit humanity

3. _____ one who studies the physical, social, and cultural development and behavior of human beings

4. _____ those who resemble humans

EXERCISE 2   Write the appropriate ANTHROP word.

1. Warren Buffett, a notable _____ and one of the richest men in the world, announced that he would donate the vast majority of his wealth to charity.

2. The _____ devoted his life to studying Mayan civilization.

3. His neighbors branded him a _____ because of his hateful attitude.

4. The gorilla's _____ features reminded Joe of his Uncle Fred.

5. The local soup kitchen is one _____ organization that fills a need in the community.

6. Many hope to change the world for the better by their _____.

7. Many children incorporate _____ when they are playing with their stuffed animals.

8. The _____ woman slammed the door on the children who were collecting for charity.

9. When we study _____, we learn about the diversity of human behavior.

10. *Sesame Street*'s Big Bird is a(n) _____ character.

EXERCISE 3 WORD LIST   Are you keeping up with your WORD LIST? Adding just a word or two each session will help you to increase your vocabulary. Remember if you use a word three times, it is yours.

EXERCISE 1 Fill in the blanks with words from the last five roots.

1. That two-headed chicken is certainly a(n) _____.

2. The _____ candidate attempted to shake the hands of everyone who attended the rally.

3. David was _____ about taking the job overseas, wanting the adventure yet dreading leaving his family and friends.

4. Luckily, our plane was _____ because we had to land on the lake.

5. Mark Twain's most humorous _____ were published in a book last year.

6. Phong is taking iron pills to alleviate his _____.

7. New City had a parade with one hundred floats to celebrate its _____ anniversary.

8. Salamanders and other _____ fascinate my younger brother.

9. Juanita and Jose celebrated their fiftieth wedding _____ with family and friends.

10. Rebecca's garden is filled with _____ flowers because she likes her plants to return each year.

11. The jury was held in the _____ before entering the courtroom.

12. The children did not _____ the long line at the movie theater.

13. When the president died in office, there was _____ in the streets until elections could be held.

14. _____ makes painful surgery possible.

15. My eighty-year-old uncle was finally _____ from his job.

EXERCISE 2 Using the following words, fill in the blanks in the paragraph so that it makes sense. Be sure to check the meaning of any words you are unsure of and add them to your WORD LIST.

ambience	annual	anteroom	atypical
amphitheater	anomaly	anticipate	biannual
ambivalent	ante	anecdotes	biennial

Yesterday was very busy for me. In the morning, I went to work at the bank, and I had to write the _____ report of the bank's financial activity. It helped that I could refer to the _____ reports from January and July. In the afternoon, I did something _____ for me: I met my girlfriend at the town's _____ to hear a local band. The show opened with the host telling _____ about how the band got its start. My girlfriend was _____ about attending but after hearing the performance, she was glad that she attended. That evening I was off to the _____ "Ninth Year Reunion" of some college friends; we meet on odd-numbered years. Part of the fun is our "Go Fish" card game. Being a social event, the _____ was only $1 per hand. After the game, we went to a restaurant whose _____ was tropical. Even in the _____, we felt as if we were on a Caribbean island. Although having a day so packed with activity is an _____ for me, I thoroughly enjoyed it, and I _____ having other fun-filled days in the near future.

EXERCISE 3 Fill in the root and its meaning for each word.

WORD	ROOT	MEANING
1. ambiguous	ambi	uncertain, two possible meanings
2. annals	_____	_____
3. anomaly	_____	_____
4. misanthropic	_____	_____
5. antecedent	_____	_____

QUIZ YOURSELF   Visit the student companion website at www.cengagebrain.com to check your progress by working with the audio flashcards.

6 ANTI—against, opposite

ANTI meaning *against* or *opposite* is easy to spot in such words as **antifreeze**, **antitrust**, and **antisocial**, but it can also help clarify more difficult words.

One ANTI word, which you probably won't have occasion to use and that won't be included in any of the tests in this book, is interesting just because of its story. **Antipodes** (an tip′ uh dez) [ANTI opposite + POD foot] means literally "with the feet opposite" and refers to any place on the *opposite* side of the Earth because the people there seem to be standing upside down with their feet *opposite* to ours. The British referred to Australia and New Zealand as the Antipodes because those countries are on the *opposite* side of the Earth.

In the following words, ANTI means *against*.

antagonist (an tag′ uh nist) [ANTI against + AGON struggle] noun—one who opposes and contends against another; an adversary; opponent. *In the Harry Potter book series, Voldemort is the antagonist.*

antagonize (an tag′ uh nīz) [ANTI against + AGON struggle] verb—to incur or provoke hostility. *Pulling its tail will antagonize the cat.*

antibiotic (an ti bi ot′ ik) [ANTI against + BIO life] noun—a substance produced by a microorganism that destroys other harmful (living) microorganisms. *Penicillin is an antibiotic that has saved millions of lives.*

antidote (an′ ti dōt) [ANTI against + DOT to give] noun—a medicine that counteracts (works against) poison or disease. *After the snake bit him, he was quickly given an antidote.* Also, something that gives protection against injurious effects. *Plentiful jobs are one of the best antidotes to crime.* Also, something that gives relief against something else. *The comedy was a pleasant antidote to all the tragedies we had seen.*

antipathy (an tip′ uh thē) [ANTI against + PATHOS feelings] noun—a strong feeling of dislike. *The coach's antipathy toward the referee was obvious to everyone in the stadium after the referee's questionable call.*

In the following words, it means *opposite*.

Antarctica (ant ark′ ti kuh) [ANTI opposite] noun—[The vowel (i) is dropped when second syllable begins with a vowel (a)] the continent opposite the Arctic. *The southernmost continent is Antarctica.*

anticlimax (an ti klī maks) noun—a sudden drop from the important to the commonplace. *Her present job as a dishwasher is an anticlimax to her brilliant career as a chef.*

antithesis (an tith′ uh sis) [ANTI opposite + THES to place] noun—the exact opposite. *Love is the antithesis of hate.* Also, ideas contrasted in balanced phrases, as *"To err is human; to forgive, divine."*

ALSO: antacid, anticlimactic, antimacassar, antiseptic, antiphonal, antitoxin, antonym (Some of these words are discussed under their other roots in the Word Index.)

EXERCISE 1 Write the correct ANTI word next to its definition.

1. _____ the continent opposite the Arctic
2. _____ a medicine that counteracts poison
3. _____ a sudden drop from importance to commonplace
4. _____ one who opposes and contends against another; an adversary
5. _____ to provoke hostility
6. _____ a substance produced by a microorganism that destroys other harmful organisms
7. _____ the exact opposite
8. _____ a strong feeling of dislike

EXERCISE 2 Write the appropriate ANTI word.

1. His dull closing speech was the _____ of his inspiring opening program.
2. Reading a good book is an _____ to boredom.
3. The man who challenged him to a fight was a powerful _____.
4. The continent of _____ surrounds the South Pole.
5. Diseases that were once fatal can now be cured with _____ (s).
6. A simple life is the _____ of a complicated one.
7. I want to keep my job, so I will not _____ my boss.
8. Most people have an _____ to liars and cheaters.

EXERCISE 3 JOURNAL Using words you have studied so far, write four sentences in your *vocabulary journal* about areas of your life that you are hopeful and/or doubtful about.

7 AUTO—self

AUTO, meaning *self*, was a common Greek root, but it took on added meaning in America in the late nineteenth century when it was applied to the new vehicle that could "move by itself"—the **automobile** [AUTO self + MOB to move].

autocracy (aw tok´ ruh sē) [AUTO self + CRAT to rule] noun—government by a single person. *The country had become an autocracy and was ripe for revolt.*

autocrat (aw´ tuh krat) [AUTO self + CRAT to rule] noun—an absolute ruler; a domineering, self-willed person. *When the autocrat took over the country, the people lost all their power.*

autocratic (aw tuh krat´ ik) [AUTO self + CRAT to rule] adjective—domineering. *The supervisor of our department is autocratic, accepting suggestions from no one.*

autograph (aw´ tuh graf) [AUTO self + GRAPH to write] verb—to write one's own name; signature. *The rock star will autograph his guitar for the charity auction.* noun—signature. *My high school yearbook is filled with my friends' autographs.*

automation (aw tuh ma´ shun) [AUTO self + MAT to act] noun—a system using self-operating machines. *The factory introduced automation, replacing many workers with robots.*

automaton (aw tom´ uh tun) [AUTO self + MAT to act] noun—an apparatus that functions by itself; a robot. Also, a person who has lost all human qualities and acts mechanically. *Because she had been stapling pages for so many hours, she felt like an automaton.*

autonomic (aw tuh nom´ ik) [AUTO self + NOM law] adjective—pertaining to the autonomic nervous system, which acts according to its own (self) laws rather than through voluntary control. It regulates the heart, digestive system, and so forth. *My beating heart is an example of the autonomic system at work.*

autonomous (aw ton´ uh mus) [AUTO self + NOM law] adjective—self-governing. *Freed from state control, the college became autonomous.*

autonomy (aw ton´ uh me) [AUTO self + NOM law] noun—the right of self-government. *Many nations under autocratic rule are struggling for autonomy.*

autopsy (aw´ top sē) [AUTO self + OP sight] noun—an examination of a dead body to discover the cause of death. *The autopsy revealed that the cause of death was heart failure.*

ALSO: autobiography, automat, automatic, automobile

EXERCISE 1 Write the appropriate AUTO word.

1. The medical examiner performed an _____ on the murder victim to determine the exact cause of death.

2. In many nations, democracy has taken the place of _____, to the benefit of the nations.

3. The islanders overthrew the dictator to achieve _____.

4. The _____ nervous system controls the heart and digestive system.

5. The director was an _____ in his control of the film, allowing others no power.

26

6. The factory worker was so tired that she appeared to be an _____.

7. After breaking away from the central governing body, the church became _____.

8. The fan asked the famous football player to _____ his ball.

9. My uncle's _____ manner frightened me when I visited him because I was used to my father's democratic ways.

10. _____ involves designing intelligent machines that can do work too dangerous for humans.

✏ **EXERCISE 2 WORD LIST**   Are you keeping up with your **WORD LIST?** Adding just a word or two each session will help you to increase your vocabulary. Remember if you use a word three times, it is yours.

✏ **EXERCISE 3 REVIEW**   Write a C in front of each sentence in which the underlined words are used correctly.

1. _____ After days of traveling across <u>Antarctica</u>, the explorers finally reached the North Pole.

2. _____ The <u>biannual</u> meeting is held in June and December.

3. _____ The secretary summarized the year's events for the society's <u>annals</u>.

4. _____ For visual variety, the interior designer arranged the pictures in an <u>asymmetrical</u> pattern.

5. _____ <u>Antiquity</u> means "in the present."

6. _____ She knew her false rumors would <u>antagonize</u> her classmates.

7. _____ The Vietnam War <u>antedates</u> World War I.

8. _____ Her <u>ambivalence</u> toward allowing her teenage son to drive caused her to change her mind by the minute.

9. _____ The elderly woman relied on her <u>annuity</u> to provide a fixed, regular income.

10. _____ An <u>agnostic</u> does not believe that there is a God.

11. _____ He presented a convincing argument against his <u>antagonist's</u> ideas.

12. _____ The mother of the slain soldier felt <u>antipathy</u> toward the government that sent him to war.

13. _____ The <u>misanthrope</u> honored the cancer society with a generous donation.

14. _____ Falsehood is the <u>antithesis</u> of truth.

15. _____ Just because a few <u>atypical</u> cells appeared, does not mean she is anemic.

8 BENE—well, good

Words that begin with BENE always describe something *good*—an action, a result, or an attitude. **Benediction** [BENE good + DICT to speak] means to speak well of, to bless, and it first came into use from saying grace before a meal.

benediction (ben uh dik′ shun) [BENE good + DICT to speak] noun—literally a speaking of good wishes; a blessing. *After the benediction, the congregation filed out.*

benefactor (ben uh fak′ tur) [BENE good + FAC to do] noun—literally one who does something good; one who gives help or financial assistance. *A generous benefactor made the well-equipped science laboratory possible.*

beneficence (buh nef′ uh suns) [BENE good + FAC to do] noun—literally the doing of good; kindness; charity. *The scholarships were funded through the beneficence of the alumni.*

beneficial (ben uh fish′ ul) [BENE well + FAC to do] adjective—producing benefits; advantageous. *Having a regular study schedule is beneficial to students.*

beneficiary (ben uh fish′ e er e) [BENE good + FAC to do] noun—a person who receives benefits, as from a will or an insurance policy. *He was the beneficiary of his father's will.*

benefit (ben′ uh fit) [BENE well + FAC to do] noun—anything that promotes well-being; a payment to one in need. *She received considerable benefits from her exercise program.*

benevolence (buh nev′ uh luns) [BENE well + VOL to wish] noun—an inclination to do good; a kindly or charitable act. *The benevolence of the sorority members was shown by their generous contributions to charity.* (Benevolence and beneficence are close synonyms.)

benevolent (buh nev′ uh lunt) [BENE well + VOL to wish] adjective—inclined to do good. *The department manager had a benevolent manner toward her staff, buying them lunch.*

benign (bi nīn′) adjective—harmless; having a kindly (good) attitude or disposition. *The parents looked upon the silly but harmless actions of their son with benign tolerance.* Also, in medicine, mild in character; not malignant. *We were thankful to learn that the growth proved to be benign rather than malignant.*

(Benevolent and benign are close synonyms. Both mean having a kindly attitude, but benevolent often includes the idea of doing something charitable, and benign often has a medical meaning opposite to malignant.)

ALSO: beneficent

✎ **EXERCISE 1** Match each **BENE** word to its definition.

1. _____ benevolent
2. _____ benediction
3. _____ benign
4. _____ beneficial
5. _____ benefactor

A. advantageous
B. inclined to do good
C. one who does good
D. a blessing
E. harmless

EXERCISE 2   Write the appropriate BENE word.

1. Nutritionists really do recommend eating "an apple a day" because apples are _____ to our health.

2. As the only child, Kelly is the sole _____ of her parents' estate.

3. The congregation rose for the _____.

4. Alec's _____ nature is obvious from his charity work.

5. The employee's medical _____ paid for his surgery.

6. The teacher's _____ provided the money for the scholarships.

7. Gina's doctor reassured her that the tumor was _____.

8. The homeless family was given shelter and food through the _____ of the charity.

9. Andrew Carnegie was the _____ whose money paid for more than 2,500 new public libraries across America.

EXERCISE 3 REVIEW   Write a C in front of each sentence in which all the words are used correctly. Then, in the remaining blanks, write the word that should have been used.

1. _____ Ten college scholarships were funded through the philanthropy of the large corporation.

2. _____ Happiness is an antagonist for political unrest.

3. _____ The anthropology class was studying the Native American Navajo culture.

4. _____ Instruments today can measure the functioning of the automaton nervous system.

5. _____ Monkeys and apes have amphibious features.

6. _____ After being a British colony for years, the island finally achieved autonomy.

7. _____ The anonymous hackers took down the website.

8. _____ Jay received a stated salary per annum plus a benefits plan.

9. _____ The song's lyrics are filled with ambiguity; listeners can interpret them in several different ways.

10. _____ The ambitious student finished her degree in three years.

EXERCISE 4 JOURNAL   Add three words to your WORD LIST that you have found difficult; then write sentences that show the meaning of each. Adding words on a regular basis to your word list as well as your journal will make a great difference in your word power.

9 BI—two

Back in the days of sailing ships, according to one story, the bread taken along on the voyages always became moldy. Then someone discovered that by baking the bread *twice*, enough moisture could be removed so that it remained edible during long voyages. The new kind of bread was called ***biscuit*** [BI two + COQUERE to cook] or *twice*-baked bread. Today, biscuits are no longer twice-baked but are merely quick breads or non-yeast breads baked in small cakes.

bicameral (bi kam´ ur ul) [BI two + CAMER chamber] adjective—composed of two legislative chambers or branches. *The United States has a bicameral legislative system composed of the Senate and the House of Representatives.*

bicentennial (bi sen ten´ ē ul) [BI two + CENT hundred + ENN year] noun—a 200th anniversary. *The United States celebrated its bicentennial in 1976.*

bicuspid (bi kus´ pid) [BI two + CUSPID point] noun—a tooth having two points. *A human adult has eight bicuspids.*

bigamy (big´ uh me) [BI two + GAM marriage] noun—marrying one person while legally married to another. *He pleaded guilty to bigamy after his two wives found out about each other.*

bilateral (bi lat´ ur ul) [BI two + LATER side] adjective—having or involving two sides; binding on both parties (in contrast to unilateral, in which only one party has an obligation). *According to the bilateral agreement, both nations agreed to a ceasefire.*

bilingual (bi ling´ gwul) [BI two + LINGU language] adjective—able to use two languages. *Worldwide, job opportunities are greater for bilingual speakers.*

bipartisan (bi pahr´ tuh zun) [BI two + PARTEM part] adjective—consisting of or supported by two parties, especially two major political parties. *Assured of bipartisan support, the senator was confident the bill would pass.*

biped (bi´ ped) [BI two + PED foot] noun—a two-footed animal. *The ostrich is the fastest and largest biped on Earth.*

bisect (bi´ sekt) [BI two + SECT to cut] verb—to cut in two, as a diameter bisects a circle. *The nature trail bisects the park.*

bivalve (bi´ valv) [BI two + VALVE hinged] noun—a mollusk having two valves or shells hinged together, as a mussel or clam. *The oyster is a bivalve that is valued by both gourmets and jewelers.*

ALSO: biannual, biceps, bicycle, biennial, bifocal, bigamist, binoculars, binomial, bipartite, biracial, biscuit

✎ EXERCISE 1   **Write the appropriate BI word.**

1. The dentist recommended a root canal for Curt's _____ because the root was infected.

2. Because her mother speaks Spanish and her father speaks English, Maya is _____.

3. In our _____ system, both the House of Representatives and the Senate must pass laws.

4. Steve, Mary's husband, committed _____ when he married Susan as well.

5. The _____ bill easily passed both houses of Congress.

6. The orchestra commemorated the _____ of Chopin's birth with a free concert.

7. Signed by both countries, the agreement was _____.

8. Both humans and birds are _____.

9. The new railroad will _____ the town's business district.

10. Bernie steamed and then ate the clam, his favorite _____.

✎ EXERCISE 2   **Underline the correctly used BI word.**

1. The United Kingdom has a (bicameral, bilingual) system of government.

2. Suri's (bivalve, bicuspid) broke when she fell off her bicycle.

3. Some computer programs allow (biped, bilingual) students to answer in either of their languages.

4. The next (bipartisan, bicentennial) celebration for the club will be in 2018.

5. The United States outlawed (bigamy, bilateral) in 1862.

6. The diameter (bisects, bipeds) the circle.

7. There was enough (bivalve, bipartisan) support in the Senate to pass the Health Reform Bill.

✎ EXERCISE 3 JOURNAL   **In your *vocabulary journal*, write five sentences that you might use if you were writing a paper about Congress. Use as many BI and BENE words as possible.**

10 BIO—life

The root BIO, meaning *life*, combines with SYM, meaning *together*, to form an interesting word—**symbiosis**, the living together of two dissimilar organisms, usually for the benefit of both. For example, the hermit crab lives among the lethal tentacles of the sea anemone and is protected from its enemies by the stinging power of the tentacles. The anemone, on the other hand, is carried in the claws or on the back of the hermit crab to new feeding grounds. Thus the symbiosis is beneficial to both.

autobiography (awt uh bī ahg′ ru fē) [AUTO self + BIO life + GRAPH to write] noun— an account of a person's life written by that person. *Benjamin Franklin's witty style and interesting life makes his autobiography an enjoyable read.*

biodegradable (bi ō di gra′ duh bul) noun—capable of being broken down by living microorganisms and absorbed by the environment. *Biodegradable detergent does not pollute the waterways.*

biofeedback (bi o fed′ bak) noun—a technique for consciously regulating a bodily (life) function thought to be involuntary, as heartbeat or blood pressure, by using an instrument to monitor the function and to signal changes in it. *She found that she could slow her pulse by using biofeedback.*

biography (bi ahg′ ru fē) [BIO life + GRAPH to write] noun—a written account of someone's life. *Carl Sandburg's biography of Abraham Lincoln, originally published in six volumes, has become the definitive chronicle of Lincoln's life.*

biology (bi ahl′ uh je) [BIO life + LOGY study of] noun—the study of plant and animal life. *Biology includes botany and zoology.*

biopsy (bi′ op sē) [BIO life + OP sight] noun—the examination of tissues removed from the living body. *The biopsy revealed that the growth was benign.*

biosphere (bi′ uh sfir) noun—the part of the Earth, extending from its crust out into the surrounding atmosphere, in which living things exist. *Airplanes fly in the biosphere.*

symbiosis (sim bē ō sis) [SYM together + BIO life] noun—the living together in close union of two dissimilar organisms, often to their mutual benefit. *The symbiosis of algae and fungi forms lichens.*

symbiotic (sim bē ot′ ik) [SYM together + BIO life] adjective—living together in a close relationship, often to the benefit of both. *Ours is a symbiotic relationship: my partner comes up with the ideas, and I put them into action.*

ALSO: antibiotic, biochemistry, bionic, microbiology

EXERCISE 1   Write the appropriate BIO word.

1. The famous actress told all her secrets in her _____.
2. Microorganisms inhabit all parts of the Earth's _____.
3. Eve and Adam have a _____ relationship: she cooks and he cleans up.
4. Many people with ADHD use _____ to relieve their symptoms.
5. Her latest book is a _____ of Raoul Wallenberg, the missing World War II hero.
6. To determine whether the tumor was benign, the doctor performed a _____.
7. Although very useful in our everyday lives, plastic is not _____.
8. The _____ of the ant and the aphid causes much distress to gardeners.
9. In my _____ class, we dissected a pig.

EXERCISE 2   Write the correct BIO word next to its definition.

1. _____ the study of plant and animal life
2. _____ a written account of someone's life
3. _____ the examination of tissues removed from the living body
4. _____ a technique for consciously regulating a bodily function by using an instrument to monitor and to signal changes in it
5. _____ an account of a person's life written by that person
6. _____ the part of the Earth, extending from its crust out into the surrounding atmosphere, in which living things exist
7. _____ capable of being broken down by living microorganisms and absorbed by the atmosphere
8. _____ the living together in close union of two dissimilar organisms, often to their mutual benefit

EXERCISE 3 JOURNAL   Write three sentences in your *vocabulary journal* about a trip to a science center using as many BIO words as you can.

EXERCISE 1 **Provide the root for each meaning. Then give a word that reflects your understanding of the root and its meaning. The first one has been done for you.**

MEANING	ROOT	WORD
1. year	ANN, ENN	annual
2. two		
3. life		
4. before		
5. not, without		
6. around, both		
7. self		
8. against, opposite		
9. well, good		
10. human		

EXERCISE 2 **Read each sentence and write a C in front of those sentences in which the underlined vocabulary words are used correctly. In the remaining blanks, write the word that should have been used.**

1. _____ The shy worker standing up and speaking at the meeting was <u>asymmetrical</u> of her.

2. _____ To <u>bivalve</u> the pie, cut it into two pieces.

3. _____ The Clean Water Act of 1972 <u>antedates</u> the Nuclear Waste Policy Act of 1982.

4. _____ Various <u>anthropomorphic</u> organizations came to the aid of the flood victims.

5. _____ Paper containers, which are <u>biodegradable</u>, help keep the landscape clean.

6. _____ Pollution is causing changes in parts of the <u>biography.</u>

7. _____ Now that she has a job and her own apartment, Christy is <u>autonomic.</u>

8. _____ We <u>synchronized</u> our watches and agreed to meet at eight o'clock A.M. sharp.

9. _____ A <u>bicentennial</u> celebration was held for the nation's 200th <u>anniversary</u>.

10. _____ Being <u>ambitious</u> has helped Ellen to succeed in her career.

EXERCISE 3 Write the letter that matches the definition with its word.

1. _____ anomaly   A. absolute ruler
2. _____ anticipate   B. by the year, annually
3. _____ antithesis   C. the study of plant and animal life
4. _____ beneficence   D. composed of two legislative chambers or branches
5. _____ biology   E. the surrounding atmosphere
6. _____ bicameral   F. resembling humans
7. _____ autocrat   G. a rare exception
8. _____ per annum   H. kindness, charity
9. _____ ambience   I. to realize beforehand
10. _____ anthropoid   J. the exact opposite

EXERCISE 4 As a review of some of the roots you have learned, make a root chain of five or more words, similar to the one on pages 1–3. Start with the word *autobiography*, and refer to the preceding pages to find the words you need.

auto bio graphy

QUIZ YOURSELF Visit the student companion website at www.cengagebrain.com to check your progress by working with the audio flashcards.

11   CEDE, CEED—go, yield, give away

The root SE, meaning *apart*, combines with the root CEDE, meaning *to go*, to form the word **secede**, which means to withdraw formally from an organization, alliance, political party, or federation. The U.S. Civil War began when first South Carolina and then the other southern states **seceded** from the Union.

antecede (an tuh sēd´) [ANTE before + CEDE go] verb—to come, go, or exist before in time, order, rank, or position. *The American Revolution antecedes the French Revolution.* (Antecede and precede have the same meaning.)

antecedent (an tuh sēd´ unt) [ANTE before + CEDE go] noun—one that goes before another; also one's ancestors. *She followed her antecedents and became a lawyer.* Also, the word, phrase, or clause that determines to what a pronoun refers. *In the sentence "The man sold his car," the word "man" is the antecedent of the pronoun "his."*

exceed (eks sēd´) [EX out + CEED go] verb—to extend beyond or outside of. *The apple on the tree exceeds her reach.*

intercede (in ter sēd´) [INTER between + CEDE go] verb—to plead on another's behalf. *The father interceded when his son got into trouble.*

precede (prē sēd´) [PRE before + CEDE go] verb—to come, go, or exist before in time, order, rank, or position. *The singing of the national anthem always precedes the start of sporting events.* (Antecede and precede have the same meaning.)

precedent (prēs´ suh dent) [PRE before + CEDE go] noun—an occurrence that is used as an example in dealing with similar instances at a later time. *The Supreme Court ruling set a precedent for fair hiring practices; now all employers must follow this precedent.*

proceed (prē sēd´) [PRO before + CEDE go] verb—to continue. *Dena will proceed with her education despite losing her financial aid.*

recede (rē sēd´) [RE back + CEDE go] verb—to move back or away from. *Every year he saw his hairline recede a bit more.*

retrocede (re trō sēd´) [RETRO back, behind + CEDE go] verb—to give back, return. *After World War II ended, Germany had to retrocede the territory it had taken during the war.*

secede (suh sēd´) [SE apart + CEDE go] verb—to withdraw formally from membership in an organization, association, political party, or alliance. *Texas was the last state to secede from the Union during the American Civil War.*

succeed (suk sēd´) [SUB next, after + CEED go] verb—to come after in time or order. *King George VI succeeded to the throne after his brother, Edward VIII, abdicated.* Also to have a favorable result. *Elaine will succeed in finishing the marathon because she practices regularly.*

✎ **EXERCISE 1   Write the correct CEDE, CEED word next to its definition.**

1. _____ one that goes before another (noun form)
2. _____ to have a favorable result
3. _____ to give back, return
4. _____ to plead on another's behalf
5. _____ to extend beyond or outside of
6. _____ to come, go, or exist before in time, order, rank, or position (verb form)
7. _____ to withdraw formally from membership in an organization, association, political party, or alliance to have a favorable result
8. _____ to move back or away from

✎ **EXERCISE 2   Write the appropriate CEDE, CEED word.**

1. Georgina's miniskirt wedding dress set a _____ among her friends.
2. Those who owned the land around what is now the Panama Canal _____ (ed) from Columbia and set up the Republic of Panama.
3. The sand _____ (s) a bit more each year from the shore's edge.
4. The lawyer _____ (ed) on his client's behalf.
5. The directions said to _____ through two traffic lights and then turn left.
6. In the alphabet, the letter "a" _____ the letter "b."
7. If you _____ the speed limit, you may get a ticket.
8. The legislature _____ (ed) the land to the Navaho tribe.
9. The orphan did not know about his _____ (s).
10. I want to _____ in learning new words, so I will study my word roots regularly.

✎ **EXERCISE 3 REVIEW   Are you adding some words to your WORD LIST? Read over your list occasionally, and try to use a few of the words in your daily conversation.**

12 CHRON—time

Like all CHRON words, **anachronism** has something to do with *time*. It is the term applied to anything that is out of its proper historical *time*. For example, it would be an anachronism to mention antibiotics when writing about the nineteenth century.

Shakespeare let several anachronisms slip into his plays. He speaks of a clock striking in *Julius Caesar*, but striking clocks had not been invented at the time of Julius Caesar. And in *King John* he mentions using cannons, but the scenes in that play took place many years before cannons were used in England.

anachronism (un nak´ ruh niz um) [ANA back + CHRON time] noun—anything out of its proper historical time. *To include a computer in a story set in 1920 would be an anachronism.*

chronic (kron´ ik) adjective—continuing for a long time, such as a chronic disease. *A chronic complainer, he was never happy with his situation.*

chronicle (kron´ i kul) noun—an account of events arranged in order of time. *Her latest book gives a chronicle of Russian history since 1910.*

chronological (kron uh loj´ i kul) adjective—arranged in order of time of occurrence. *A biography is usually written in chronological order.*

chronology (kruh nol´ uh je) [CHRON time + -LOGY study of] noun—a list of events arranged according to time of occurrence. *For history class he had to memorize the chronology of the reigns of the English monarchs.*

chronometer (kruh nom´ uh tur) [CHRON time + METER measure] noun—a precision instrument that measures time, such as a clock, a watch, or an instrument used for marine navigation. *Before making an entry in the log, the captain consulted the chronometer.*

synchronize (sin´ kruh nīz) [SYN together + CHRON time] verb—to cause to operate (keep time) in unison, as to synchronize watches (chronometers) or to synchronize the sound with the film in a motion picture. *The sound track of the film was not synchronized with the picture so those of us in the movie theater complained.*

✎ **EXERCISE 1 JOURNAL**   Write three sentences in your *vocabulary journal* using as many CHRON words as you can. Be sure each sentence shows the word's meaning. Writing in your *vocabulary journal* on a regular basis will make a great difference in your word power.

✎ **EXERCISE 2**   Write the correct CHRON next to its definition.

1. _____ arranged in order of time of occurrence
2. _____ continuing for a long time
3. _____ to cause to operate (keep time) in unison
4. _____ anything out of its proper historical time
5. _____ an instrument for measuring time precisely
6. _____ an account of events arranged in order of time
7. _____ a list of events arranged according to time of occurrence

✎ **EXERCISE 3**   Write the appropriate CHRON word.

1. The lawyer asked the witness to give a _____ of the events.
2. The smoker had a _____ cough.
3. Let's _____ the dance movements with the beat of the music.
4. The handmade Swiss _____ was accurate to the second.
5. I find it easier to learn history when it is taught in _____ order.
6. With his breech pants and coonskin hat, Jared was considered a(n) _____ by his neighbors.
7. Robert wrote a _____ of his family's history.

13 CIRCUM—around

CIRCUM always means *around*. A **circumference** is the outer boundary line *around* a circular area. To **circumnavigate** the globe is to go *around* it. **Circumlocution** is a *roundabout* way of saying something. What are the **circumstances** *around* your interest in increasing your vocabulary?

circuit (sur´ kit) [CIRCUM around] noun—the regular journey around a territory by a person performing duties. *The newspaper carrier made his daily circuit through the city's streets.* Also, a closed path followed by an electric current. *When the circuit was interrupted, the lights went out.* Also, an arrangement of electrically or electromagnetically connected components. *Computers use integrated circuits.*

circuitous (sur kyO´ uh tus) [CIRCUM around] adjective—roundabout; winding. *Because she didn't know the way, she took us by a rather circuitous route. His speech was full of circuitous arguments that led nowhere.*

circumference (sur kum´ furnts) [CIRCUM around + FER to carry] noun—the outer boundary line around a circular area. *In our math class, we learned how to find the circumference of a circle.*

circumlocution (sur kum lō kyO´ shun) [CIRCUM around + LOC to speak] noun—a roundabout way of saying something. *Saying "A number of other commitments will make it impossible for me to find the time to attend the meeting" would be a circumlocution for the simple statement "I can't attend the meeting."*

circumnavigate (sur kum nav´ uh gāt) [CIRCUM around + NAV to sail] verb—to sail around. *Magellan was the first person to circumnavigate the globe.*

circumscribe (sur´ kum skrīb) [CIRCUM around + SCRIB to write] verb—to limit; to confine. *The rules of the private school circumscribe the daily activities of the students.*

circumspect (sur´ kum spekt) [CIRCUM around + SPEC to look] adjective—cautious; careful to consider possible consequences. *She was circumspect in making suggestions to her temperamental boss.*

circumstance (sur´ kum stants) [CIRCUM around + STA to stand] noun—a fact or an event accompanying another fact or event. *Because of circumstances at home, I had to give up the trip I had planned.*

circumvent (sur kum vent´) [CIRCUM around + VEN to come] verb—to get around or to overcome by clever maneuvering; to prevent. *By offering a small wage increase, the management hoped to circumvent a walkout.*

✐ **EXERCISE 1   Write the appropriate CIRCUM word.**

1. Using _____ in your speech only confuses your listeners.

2. Magellan _____ the horn of South Africa.

3. The college's administrators plan to _____ the students' protests by raising tuition five percent instead of the planned ten percent.

4. The letter carrier's _____ took him four hours to complete.

5. Bloggers should be _____ when posting a story that may be damaging.

6. The _____ footpath seemed to go on forever.

7. Because of his new job, Wei's financial _____ improved greatly.

8. My mother's rules were meant to _____ our mischievous behavior.

9. The _____ of the jogging circle is exactly one mile.

✐ **EXERCISE 2   What words using the root CIRCUM are associated with the following definitions?**

1. _____ to limit, to confine

2. _____ to get around or to overcome by clever maneuvering

3. _____ the regular journey around a territory by a person performing duties

4. _____ a roundabout way of saying something

5. _____ to sail around

6. _____ a fact or an event accompanying another fact or event

7. _____ cautious; careful to consider possible consequences

8. _____ the outer boundary line around a circular area

9. _____ roundabout; winding

✐ **EXERCISE 3 JOURNAL   Write three sentences in your *vocabulary journal* about a trip you would like to take using as many CIRCUM words as you can.**

EXERCISE 4 WORD LIST   Are you keeping up with your WORD LIST. Adding just a word or two each session will help you to increase your vocabulary. Remember if you use a word three times, it is yours.

14 COGNI, GNOS—to know

If you **recognize** [RE again + COGNI know] someone, you *know* him or her again. COGNI is the Latin root for *know*; the Greek root for *know* is GNOS. From *gnos* we get ***gnostic***, meaning divine knowledge, particularly of God, so an ***agnostic*** [A not + GNOS to know] is someone who does not know whether there is a God. If you are ill, you get a ***diagnosis*** [DIA by, through + GNOS know], through your doctor's knowledge. You may not ***recognize*** the word acquaint, meaning *toward knowing*, as having a COGNI root because over time and through use, its spelling has changed.

cognitive (kog´ ni tiv) [COGNI to know] adjective—relating to or involving conscious intellectual activity, such as thinking, reasoning, or remembering. *We worried that his head injury would impair his cognitive ability.*

cognizant (kog´ ni zent) [COGNI to know] adjective—knowledgeable or understanding of something; fully informed. *The police officer was cognizant of his responsibility to the community that he served.*

diagnosis (di´ eg nō´ sis) [DIA apart + COGNI to know] noun—investigation or analysis of the cause or nature of a condition, situation, or problem. *The X-ray confirmed the diagnosis of a broken leg.*

diagnostic (di´ eg nos´ tik) [DIA apart + COGNI to know] adjective—a distinguishing sign or symptom; using the methods of or yielding a diagnosis. *The mechanic ran a diagnostic test on the car to determine why it was running roughly.*

incognito (in kog nē´ tō) [IN not + COGNI to know] adjective or adverb—with one's identity concealed or disguised. *The spy traveled incognito.*

metacognition (me´ ta kog´ ni shun) [META beyond, change + COGNI to know] noun—knowledge or awareness about one's own learning or thinking processes. *The study skills teacher told the students to practice metacognition when reading their textbook.*

prognosis (prog nō´ sis) [PRO forward, forth + GNOS to know] noun—literally foreknowledge; a forecast or prediction usually associated with the prospect of recovery, such as from a disease. *The prognosis for her recovery was good.*

prognosticate (prog nos´ ti kāt) [PRO forward, forth + GNOS to know] verb—literally sign of the future; a forecast or prediction. *The researcher explained that science does not prognosticate.*

recognition (rek eg nish´ un) [RE back, again + COGNI to know] noun—knowledge that someone or something present has been encountered before. *Her recognition of faces from long ago is exceptional.*

ALSO: agnostic, cognoscente, diagnose, ignorance, ignorant, precognition, recognize, recognizance

✎ **EXERCISE 1** **Write the correct COGNI, GNOS word next to its definition.**

1. _____ knowledgeable or understanding of something; fully informed

2. _____ knowledge that someone or something present has been encountered before

3. _____ with one's identity concealed or disguised

4. _____ awareness or analysis of one's own learning or thinking processes

5. _____ investigation or analysis of the cause or nature of a condition, situation, or problem

6. _____ a forecast or prediction

7. _____ relating to or involving conscious intellectual activity

8. _____ literally, to forecast or predict, usually associated with the prospect of recovery

✎ **EXERCISE 2** **Write the appropriate COGNI, GNOS word.**

1. Rachel's superior _____ ability is reflected in her high grades.

2. Although he was very sick, his _____ for a full recovery was good.

3. X-rays are a _____ tool used to detect broken bones.

4. Robins hopping in the yard _____ spring.

5. Her doctor's _____ of diabetes made her change her eating and exercise habits.

6. The buyer for the department store was _____ of her responsibility to balance style and price.

7. Students who use their _____ perform better on exams and complete their work more efficiently than students who don't.

8. The famous movie star attended the concert _____.

✎ **EXERCISE 3 JOURNAL** **Write three sentences in your *vocabulary journal* about an obstacle you have overcome using as many COGNI, GNOS words as you can.**

15 COM, CON, COL, COR—together, with

Companion takes on new meaning when we learn its roots. A companion [COM with + PAN bread] was originally a person one shared one's bread *with*. We don't think of that original meaning today, and yet when we want to be hospitable, we invite our companions to share our food.

COM, meaning *together* or *with*, is sometimes difficult to spot because it so often changes its last letter to be like the first letter of the root following it. Thus COMloquial becomes COLloquial, COMnect becomes CONnect, and COMrelate becomes CORrelate. Sometimes the letter *m* is dropped completely, and COMeducation becomes COeducation. Changing the last letter in these ways makes pronunciation easier. Sometimes, as in **condone** and **compunction**, COM is used merely as an intensive, giving more emphasis to the root that follows.

On page 5 is a further discussion of changes in root spelling.

coherent (ko hir´ unt) [CO together + HER to stick] adjective—literally sticking together; having an orderly relation of parts. *My geology professor's lectures are always coherent and interesting.*

collaborate (kuh lab´ uh rāt) [COL together + LABOR work] verb—to labor together. *Students learn better when they collaborate on their studies.*

collusion (kuh lO´ zhun) [COL together + LUD to play] noun—a secret agreement between two or more persons for a deceitful purpose. *The manager suspected collusion between the two employees accused of embezzling company funds.*

commensurate (kuh men´ suh rit) [COM together + METR to measure] adjective—equal in measure or size; proportionate. *The pay should be commensurate with the work.*

commiserate (kuh miz´ uh rāt) [COM with + MISERARI to pity] verb—to sympathize. *My sister commiserated with me over my bad math grade.*

commotion (kuh mo´ shun) [COM together + MOT to move] noun—people moving together; social disorder. *The commotion disrupted the meeting.*

compunction (kum pungk´ shun) [COM (intensive) + PUNCT to prick] noun—an uneasiness caused by a sense of guilt; a slight regret. *He felt compunction about lying to his mother.*

concur (kun kur´) [COM together + CUR to run] verb—to express agreement, to be of the same opinion. *Experts on health care concur that patients must be involved in their treatment.*

condone (kun don´) [COM (intensive) + DON to give] verb—to forgive or overlook (an offense). *The teacher condoned the silly behavior of his class on the day before summer vacation.*

congenital (kun jen´ uh tul) [CON together + GEN birth] adjective—existing at birth. *The child has a congenital heart defect.*

consensus (kun sen´ sus) [CON together + SENS to feel] noun—general agreement. *Consensus has been reached about the importance of reading to children.*

consummate (kun sum´ it) [CON together + SUMMA sum] adjective—complete, perfect, or utter in every respect or manner. *She was a consummate artist.*

convene (kun ven´) [CON together + VEN to come] verb—to come together formally. *The committee will convene next week.*

convivial (kun viv´ ē ul) [CON together + VIV to live] adjective—fond of eating, drinking, and being sociable together. *In a convivial mood, the guests stayed until midnight.*
correlate (kor´ uh lāt) verb—to relate together; to show relationship. *The accountant is trying to correlate this year's figures with last year's.*

ALSO: colloquial, colloquium, complacent, complicate, composition, compulsive, concoction, concord, concourse, concurrent, conducive, congregation, conjugal, conscription, contemporary, conversant, corrupt

EXERCISE 1   Write the appropriate COM, CON, COL, COR word.

1. The drunkard's rambling explanation was not _____.

2. The warden realized that the guard was in _____ with the inmate.

3. The thief felt no _____ about stealing the painting.

4. He is the _____ athlete, winning the Heisman Trophy.

5. The child's running around caused a _____ at the restaurant.

6. The Windsor Book Club is a _____ group whose meetings are well attended.

7. I _____ with Thomas Jefferson's point that our republic should "secure to all its citizens a perfect equality of rights."

8. The artist and the writer _____ (ed) on the website's visuals and content.

9. Refusing to _____ her son's rude behavior, the mother sent him to time out.

10. The children's allowance is _____ with their chores.

11. Both of the researchers' findings _____ to a high degree of accuracy.

12. A _____ was reached by the council after hours of discussion.

13. The court will _____ at noon to decide the case.

14. The deformity of Jonah's spine is not _____, but the result of an accident in infancy.

15. They _____ (d) with him over his loss of the bicycle race.

EXERCISE 2 JOURNAL   In your *vocabulary journal*, write a few sentences describing a party. Use as many of your COM, CON, COL, COR vocabulary words as possible.

✎ **EXERCISE 3   Underline the appropriate COM, CON, COL, COR word.**

1. His rate of promotion is (commensurate, consensus) with his hard work.

2. The manager does not (correlate, condone) sloppy work.

3. Her IQ score and her grades did not (correlate, collaborate).

4. I felt no (compunction, commotion) about missing that meeting.

5. Her sympathetic friends were more than willing to (concur, commiserate) with her about her lost puppy.

6. The (collusion, consensus) of the committee was that more funds were necessary to support the school's athletic programs.

7. The two scientists will (collaborate, condone) on the project.

8. The child's inability to hear was traced to a (coherent, congenital) defect.

9. Upset, the driver was unable to give a (convivial, coherent) account of the accident.

10. The board members will (convene, commiserate) on June 1 to discuss the matter.

✎ **EXERCISE 4 WORD LIST   Remember to keep up with your WORD LIST. Adding just a word or two each session will help you to increase your vocabulary.**

EXERCISE 1 Match the word with its definition. Look for clues to each word's meaning in the word's root.

1. _____ antecedent	**A.**	continuing for a long time
2. _____ circumnavigate	**B.**	producing benefits; advantageous
3. _____ chronic	**C.**	one that goes before another
4. _____ bigamy	**D.**	an apparatus that functions by itself; a robot
5. _____ beneficial	**E.**	marrying one person while legally married to another
6. _____ automaton	**F.**	to continue
7. _____ proceed	**G.**	a sudden drop from the important to the commonplace
8. _____ anticlimax	**H.**	to sail around
9. _____ anthropoid	**I.**	knowledgeable or understanding of something
10. _____ cognizant	**J.**	resembling humans

EXERCISE 2 REVIEW Using the following nine words, fill in the blanks in the paragraph so that it makes sense. After you check your answers online, reread the paragraph and see how satisfying it is to read a paragraph in which you are sure of all the words.

biodegradable	circuitous	biology
amphibians	compunction	condone
perennial	bivalves	ambivalent

Last weekend our _____ class went to the ocean to study

_____ , _____, and various other

forms of marine life. On our way there, we took a _____ route

through a wooded area and were dismayed to find the roadside cluttered with bottles, plastic

cartons, and other trash that isn't _____. People like a beautiful

countryside, yet they litter. They seem _____ about our natural

scenery. They wouldn't _____ messiness in their own backyards,

yet they feel no _____ about tossing a bottle or candy wrapper

into the woods. It is a _____ problem, and it will be solved only

when each individual develops a responsible attitude toward our natural scenery.

QUIZ YOURSELF   Visit the student companion website at www.cengagebrain.com to check your progress by working with the audio flashcards.

16 CRED—to believe

In the Middle Ages, it was customary for servants to carry the prepared food from the kitchen to a small side table in the dining hall, where, in front of the master and his guests, one of the servants would taste the food to show that it was not spoiled or poisoned. This side table came to be called a **credence** (belief or trust), and today in France, a side table is still called a *crédence* and in Italy a *credenza*. Today in the United States, a side table is sometimes called a *credenza*. Our English word **credence** no longer refers to our trust in the food we eat, but we still speak of having credence (belief or trust) in what we read and in what people tell us.

Note how the following CRED words go in pairs:

credible—believable
incredible—unbelievable

credulous—believing too readily
incredulous—not believing readily

credulity—tendency to believe readily
incredulity—tendency not to believe readily

credence (kre′ duns) noun—belief; acceptance as true. *They should not have given any credence to the rumor.*

credentials (kri den′ shuls) noun—documents that cause others to believe in one. *The credentials the teacher brought from her last job were excellent.*

credibility (kred uh bil′ uh tē) noun—trustworthiness. *No one ever questioned the candidate's credibility.*

credible (kred′ uh bul) adjective—believable. *He gave a credible explanation for his tardiness.*

credit (kred′ ut) noun—trust, as financial credit; a source of honor, as a credit to one's family. *My sister always paid cash rather than using her credit card.*

credulity (kri dO′ li tē) noun—tendency to believe readily on too little evidence; gullibility. *Her credulity made her easy prey for anyone with a hard luck story.*

credulous (krej′ uh lus) adjective—believing too readily on too little evidence; gullible. *Only a credulous person would be taken in by such ads.*

creed (krēd) noun—a formal statement of religious or other belief, as the creed of a church. *The young boy learned to repeat the Apostles' Creed in religion class.*

discredit (dis kred′ ut) [DIS not + CRED to believe] verb—literally not to believe; to distrust; to destroy belief in. *Because the newspaper articles had discredited the CEO of the company, he resigned.*

incredible (in kred′ uh bul) [IN not + CRED to believe] adjective—unbelievable. *Carl Lewis's Olympic relay run of 8.80 seconds was an incredible feat.*

incredulity (in kri dO′ li tē) [IN not + CRED to believe] noun—tendency not to believe readily; skepticism. *As the teacher listened to his students' excuses, his incredulity was obvious.*

incredulous (in krej′ uh lus) [IN not + CRED to believe] adjective—not believing readily; disbelieving. *When the singer heard she had won the prize, she was incredulous.*

miscreant (mis′ krē unt) [MIS less + CRED to believe] noun—originally, an unbeliever in religion; now, an evildoer or criminal. *Instead of just catching and punishing miscreants, we should focus on educating them.*

ALSO: accreditation, accredited, creditor

✎ EXERCISE 1   Write the appropriate CRED word.

1. When his parents learned that their son had eloped with a woman he had just met, they were _____.

2. On our two-week trek through the woods, we had some _____ adventures, including avoiding a bear.

3. The _____ has so far evaded the police.

4. The _____ witness gave important testimony to win the case.

5. His spending habits have marked him as a poor _____ risk.

6. All visitors have to produce _____ before they are allowed to enter the country.

7. The defense attorney tried to _____ the prosecution's witness.

8. I wouldn't give any _____ to such a poorly documented story.

9. Because Hogan has always told the truth, his _____ should not be questioned.

10. I'm not so _____ as to believe all I am told.

11. Girl Scouts recite the organization's _____ at the start of each meeting.

12. My grandmother's _____ made her an easy target for pranksters.

13. The students expressed _____ at the principal's numerous new rules.

✎ EXERCISE 2   Write the correct CRED word next to its definition.

1. _____ unbelievable

2. _____ to distrust

3. _____ not believing readily

4. _____ an evildoer or criminal

5. _____ a formal statement of one's religious or other belief

6. _____ belief; accepting as true

✎ EXERCISE 3   Underline the appropriate CRED word.

1. Because her (credit, creed) was excellent, the bank manager approved her loan.

2. The fans reacted with (credible, incredulity) at the umpire's poor calls.

3. The visiting lecturer's (miscreant, credentials) are top-notch.

4. The dean of students reacted with (discredit, credulity) upon hearing the story.

5. Her personal (credibility, credit) has served her well throughout her life.

17 CUR—to run

If you find it difficult to hang on to your money, don't be surprised—the word **currency** literally means *running*. The currency in circulation in a country is constantly *running* from person to person. And if currency should *run* through the hands of a person or a company too rapidly, it might be the **precursor** [PRE before + CUR to run] or forerunner of bankruptcy.

concourse (kon′ kors) [CON together + CUR to run] noun—a large open space where crowds gather. *The main concourse in the airport was filled with tourists.*

concur (kon kur′) [CON together + CUR to run] verb—to agree. *The faculty concurs with the recommendation of the committee.*

concurrent (kun kur′ unt) [CON together + CUR to run] adjective—literally running together; occurring at the same time. *The town council and the school board held concurrent meetings.*

courier (kur′ ē ur) [CUR to run] noun—one who carries (runs with) messages. *The courier arrived with the letter.*

current (kur′ unt) [CUR to run] noun—the flow (running) of water, air, or electricity; prevalent at the moment (running along), as current fashions. *The current trend is toward electric cars.*

curriculum (kuh rik′ yuh lum) [CUR to run] noun— all the courses offered by an educational institution. *The curriculum includes the study of the natural sciences, the social sciences, and the humanities, which are all required for a well-rounded education.*

cursive (kur′ siv) [CUR to run] adjective—handwriting with the letters joined together. *She preferred to print rather than write in cursive.*

cursory (kur′ suh re)—[CUR to run] adjective—running over rapidly without attention to detail; hasty and superficial. *The book reviewer gave the novel only a cursory reading.*

discourse (dis′ kors) [DIS apart + CUR to run] noun—to speak at length; a formal and lengthy discussion of a subject. *The instructor gave a discourse on Ibsen's symbolism.*

excursion (ik skur′ zhun) [EX out + CUR to run] noun—literally a running out somewhere; a short journey. *We took a day's excursion down the river.*

precursor (pri kur′ sur) [PRE before + CUR to run] noun—a person or thing that runs before; a forerunner. *The fountain pen was the precursor of the ballpoint pen.*

recourse (re′ kors) [RE back + CUR to run] noun—literally a running back (for help); a turning to or seeking help, safety or aid. *Violence should never be one's first recourse.*

recur (ri kur′) [RE again + CUR to run] verb—to happen again. *If the problem with your car battery should recur, you'll have to buy a new one.*

recurrent (ri kur′ unt) [RE back + CUR to run] adjective—appearing or occurring again or periodically. *Lisa's recurrent infections worried her doctor.*

ALSO: concurrence, corridor, course, currency, incur, incursion, occur, occurrence

✎ **EXERCISE 1   Write the correct CUR word next to its definition.**

1. _____ the courses offered by an educational institution
2. _____ handwriting with the letters joined together
3. _____ a forerunner
4. _____ to speak at length
5. _____ one who carries messages
6. _____ to happen again

✎ **EXERCISE 2   Write the appropriate CUR word.**

1. Because the two graduation parties were _____, Stan had to choose which one to attend.

2. Her day-long _____ to the mountains made her feel as if she had vacationed for a week.

3. French schoolchildren learn to write in _____ while in kindergarten.

4. The swift _____ carried our raft down the river.

5. Most colleges include a core _____ of English, math, and science.

6. If you don't understand an assignment, your best _____ is to ask your teacher.

7. His _____ attacks of asthma convinced him to see a specialist.

8. I _____ with your suggestions and will recommend them to the group.

9. I was surprised that he gave the important document only a _____ reading.

10. Hundreds of waiting passengers filled the train's _____.

11. Our company uses a bicycle _____ to deliver our messages in the city.

12. The visiting lecturer's _____ on new practices in criminology fascinated the audience.

13. Thunder and lightning is usually the _____ to a storm.

14. The teenager's acne _____ (red) so she will have to go for treatment again.

✎ **EXERCISE 3 JOURNAL   In your *vocabulary journal*, write four sentences about a track-and-field meet. Use as many of your CUR vocabulary words as possible.**

18 DEM—people

Many words have changed their meanings over the centuries, some having changed so much that they now mean almost the opposite of what they meant originally. **Demagogue** is an example.

First used at the time of the Peloponnesian War, the word demagogue (DEM people + AGOG leader) referred to a leader or orator who championed the cause of the common *people* of Athens in their fight against the aristocrats of Sparta. Gradually through the years, however, such leaders began pursuing their own interests rather than helping the people, and today a demagogue is a corrupt political leader who makes impassioned appeals to the emotions and prejudices of *people* to gain personal power.

demagogue (dem´ uh gog) [DEM people + AGOG leader] noun—a leader who stirs up the people by appealing to their emotions and prejudices to win them over quickly and thus gain power often advocating violence. *Adolph Hitler was the consummate demagogue.*

demagoguery (dem´ uh gog uh re) [DEM people + AGOG leader] noun—the methods or practices of a demagogue, one who stirs up the people by appealing to their emotions and prejudices to win them over quickly and thus gain power. *Hitler's campaign speeches in 1930s Germany were pure demagoguery.*

democracy (di mahk´ ru sē) [DEM people + CRAC to rule] noun—literally people rule; government by representatives elected by the people. *When the townspeople directly voted on the library budget, democracy worked.*

democratic (dem uh krat´ ik) [DEM people + CRAC to rule] adjective—of, for, or appealing to people; advocating or supporting democracy. *The newly formed country wrote its constitution based on democratic principles.*

demographic (dem uh graf´ ik) [DEM people + GRAPH to write] adjective—literally writing about people; about the study of human populations, especially their density, distribution, and vital statistics. *The government collects important demographic information about its citizens, including gender, age, race, and socioeconomic status.*

endemic (en dem´ ik) [EN in + DEM people] adjective—native to a particular people or country, as an endemic disease, which occurs only among certain people, or an endemic plant or animal, which is found only in a certain location. *The snail darter, an endangered species, is endemic to the Little Tennessee River.*

epidemic (ep uh dem´ ik) [EPI upon + DEM people] noun—a disease or other abnormal condition spreading rapidly among many people. *The flu epidemic caused many absences from work.*

pandemic (pan dem´ ik) [PAN all + DEM people] adjective or noun—literally among all the people; widespread. *The Great Depression of the 1930s was pandemic.*

ALSO: democrat, demography

EXERCISE 1   **Write the appropriate DEM word.**

1. Hitler's _____ is one cause of World War II.
2. Because of the vaccination program, the citizens no longer fear a smallpox _____.
3. _____ information is essential to choosing a business location.
4. The newly formed government was proud to be a _____.
5. The eucalyptus tree was _____ to Australia, but now it can be found in many parts of the world.
6. The councilman is a _____, seeking only to advance his own career.
7. The "Spanish Flu" of 1917–1918 was _____, causing more deaths than World War I.
8. The president of the club favored a _____ process that allowed all the members to express their opinions.

EXERCISE 2   **Write the DEM word next to its definition.**

1. _____ native to a particular people or country
2. _____ widespread
3. _____ government by representatives elected by the people
4. _____ a disease or other abnormal condition spreading rapidly among many people
5. _____ about the study of human populations, especially their density, distribution, and vital statistics

EXERCISE 3 JOURNAL   **Write several sentences in your *vocabulary journal* about your favorite period in history using some of the CRED, CUR, and DEM words you have learned. Check the sentence given in the explanation of each word to make sure you are using the word correctly.**

19 DICT—to speak

The word **addict** has a long history. In Roman law, to addict a person meant to turn that person over to a master by sentence (*speaking*) of the court. Through the years, addict has kept something of its old meaning in that it now refers to turning oneself over to a habit, which can, of course, be a master.

abdicate (ab´ di kāt) [AB away + DICT to speak, proclaim] verb—to renounce formally a throne or high office. *Pope Benedict XVI abdicated the papal office in 2013.*

contradict (kahn tru dikt´) [CONTRA against + DICT to speak] verb—to speak against; to assert the opposite of what someone has said. *I didn't dare contradict her; she was a pure demagogue.*

dictate (dik´ tāt) verb—to speak or read something aloud to be recorded by another; to give (speak) orders or commands. *The boss dictates his messages into his smartphone.*

dictator (dik´ tēt ur) noun—one whose speech is to be taken as the final word; one who orders others around; a tyrannical ruler. *Cuba has been ruled by a dictator for over sixty years.*

dictatorial (dik tu tor´ ē ul) adjective—speaking and acting in a domineering or oppressive way. *The crew resented the dictatorial manner of the foreman.*

diction (dik´ shun) noun—choice of words in speaking or writing. *She used excellent diction, always choosing exactly the right word.* Also, enunciation in speaking or singing. *His diction was so clear that he could be understood at the back of the auditorium.*

dictionary (dik´ shu ner ē) noun—a book containing the words, definitions, parts of speech, and etymology of a (spoken) language. *When I study a foreign language, I always make sure I have my dictionary close by.*

edict (ē ´ dikt) [E out + DICT to speak] noun—literally a speaking out; an official decree. *In 1598, Henry IV issued the Edict of Nantes, granting toleration to Protestants in France.*

jurisdiction (joor us dik´ shun) [JURIS law + DICT to speak] noun—the right to interpret (speak) and apply the law; legal power to hear and decide cases; geographical area. *The sheriff's jurisdiction included the city and the county surrounding it.*

predict (pri dikt´) [PRE before + DICT to speak] verb—literally to speak beforehand; to forecast or foretell. *The sportscaster predicted a successful season for the home team.*

valedictorian (val uh dik tor´ ē un) [VALE farewell + DICT to speak] noun—a student, usually of the highest scholastic standing, who gives the farewell speech at commencement. *The valedictorian gave an inspiring speech at graduation.*

ALSO: addict, addiction, benediction, dictum, ditto, interdict, malediction, verdict

✎ **EXERCISE 1 JOURNAL** In your *vocabulary journal*, write a few sentences using your DICT words about what you have read in the news. Pick the words you are unfamiliar with.

✎ **EXERCISE 2   Write the appropriate DICT word.**

1. When Edward VII _____ (ed) his throne to marry the divorced Mrs. Simpson, the world was shocked.

2. The chef _____ (ed) that night's menu to his wait staff.

3. The large number of cases in her _____ overwhelmed the judge.

4. Because I have the highest grade point average, I am the _____ of my class.

5. The foreign student took classes to improve his _____.

6. The teacher's _____ attitude never allows her students to voice their opinions.

7. Based on his improved study habits, Sanjay _____ (s) he will have a successful semester.

8. The king's _____ granted all citizens the right to own property.

9. The _____ brought tyranny to the people of his country.

10. The evidence will either affirm or _____ his story.

11. In 1806, Noah Webster published the first American _____.

✎ **EXERCISE 3 REVIEW   Give the root and two words from the root for each meaning.**

MEANING	ROOT	WORD
1. people	_____	_____
2. around	_____	_____
3. know	_____	_____
4. self	_____	_____
5. to run	_____	_____
6. together, with	_____	_____
7. well, good	_____	_____
8. time	_____	_____
9. against, opposite	_____	_____
10. life	_____	_____
11. year	_____	_____
12. to believe	_____	_____
13. go, give way, yield	_____	_____

20 DIS, DI, DIF—not, away, apart

In Roman times it was important to start a journey or begin a new venture on a lucky day. One way to find out whether a day was favorable was to consult the stars. If the stars were *not* in a favorable position, the outcome of any undertaking begun on that day was certain to be a **disaster** (DIS not + ASTER star).

diffident (dif´ eh dent) [DIF away + FID trust] adjective—not having faith in oneself; shy; timid. *The foreign student was too diffident to make friends with Americans.*

diffuse (dif use´) [DIF away + FUSE to pour] adjective—spread out or disbursed; not concentrated. *The photographer diffused the light to get his desired effect.*

disarray (dis uh rā´) [DIS not + AREER to array] noun—a state of disorder or confusion; disorderly dress. *Following the death of their leader, the political group fell into disarray.*

disburse (dis burs´) [DIS away + BURSA a purse] verb—literally to take away from a purse; to pay out, as from a fund. *The president of the society disbursed the scholarship funds.*

disconcert (dis kun surt´) [DIS not + CONCERT to bring into agreement] verb—to upset; to frustrate. *The guest speaker was disconcerted by the loud, rude students.*

disconsolate (dis kon´ suh lit) verb—not able to be consoled; hopelessly sad. *The team member responsible for losing the relay was disconsolate.*

discordant (dis kor´ dunt) [DIS apart + CORD heart] adjective—not in agreement or harmony. *One discordant voice can ruin a choir.*

disparity (di spar´ uh tē) [DIS not + PAR equal] noun—difference; unlikeness; unequal. *Despite the disparity in their ages, they get along well.*

disproportionate (dis pruh por´ shun it) noun—not proportionate; out of proportion in size, shape, or amount. *His salary was disproportionate to the amount of work he did.*

dissect (dī´ sekt) [DIS apart + SECT to cut] verb—to cut apart, especially for anatomical study. *Our biology class dissected frogs yesterday.*

disseminate (di sem´ uh nāt) [DIS apart + SEMIN seed] verb—to spread abroad as if sowing seed. *The publication disseminated information about endangered species.*

dissent (di sent´) [DIS apart + SENT to feel] verb—to differ in opinion or feeling; to withhold approval. *If too many members dissent, the motion will not pass.*

dissident (dis´ uh dunt) [DIS apart + SID to sit] noun—literally sitting apart; one who disagrees. *The dissidents made trouble for the ruling party.*

dissuade (di swād´) [DIS away + SUAD to persuade] verb—to turn a person away from a course of action or statement by means of persuasion. *His coworkers dissuaded him from giving up his job until he found a better one.*

diverse (di vurs´) [DI away + VERS to turn] adjective—differing from one another; unlike, as in distinct opinions; differing in character, form or kind. *New York is a culturally diverse city.*

ALSO: discomfit, discord, discourse, discredit, discrepancy, discursive, dismantle, dismiss, disparage, disparate, dispel, dispense, disrupt, dissolution, dissonant, distort, diversity, divert, diversion

✎ **EXERCISE 1**   **Write the appropriate DIS, DI, DIF word.**

1. Kathy woke up, looked at the time, and sped out the door, her hair and clothes in
   _____.

2. The _____ toddler will not leave his mother's side.

3. The _____ sunlight brightened the whole room.

4. The college took out newspaper and radio advertisements to _____
   the information about its new campus.

5. Her _____ singing kept the carolers from enjoying the evening.

6. The _____ between what she expected for her birthday and what
   she received was enormous.

7. The club members agreed on how to _____ their funds.

8. Our national deficit is _____ to tax revenues received.

9. The lone _____ was ignored during the budget meeting.

10. Leaders of the D.A.R.E. program hope to _____ youngsters
    from using illegal drugs.

✎ **EXERCISE 2**   **Match each word with its definition.**

A. dissect   C. dissident   E. disconsolate

B. diverse   D. disconcert   F. disproportionate

1. _____ unlike; differing in character, form or kind

2. _____ not able to be consoled; hopelessly sad

3. _____ one who disagrees; a dissenter

4. _____ to cut apart

5. _____ to upset; frustrate

6. _____ out of proportion in size, shape, or amount

✎ **EXERCISE 3 JOURNAL**   **In your *vocabulary journal*, write three sentences
about a lecture that you have attended. You may use any of the words you have
studied so far.**

EXERCISE 4   Using the following words, fill in the blanks in the paragraph so that it makes sense. After you check your answers online, reread the paragraph and see how satisfying it is to read a paragraph in which you are sure of all the words.

disburse	disparity	diverse
dissuade	disarray	disproportionate
dissent	disconsolate	

Madeline was in a _____ mood because the house was in

_____. Madeline shared the house with four other students, who

were a _____ group composed of men, women, freshman, senior,

and from several different cultures. Alexa felt she did a _____

share of the housework while Tariq thought there was a _____

in the amount of mess each one made. In response, Chen suggested they start a household

fund and _____ the monies to a housekeeper each week. Zach-

ary tried to _____ his housemates from hiring a housekeeper, say-

ing they should clean up after themselves. But when a vote was taken, he was the only one

to _____, so the group decided to hire a housekeeper to solve their

cleaning problems.

EXERCISE 5 REVIEW   As a review of some of the roots you have learned, make a root chain similar to the one on pages 1–3. Start with *concur* and refer to the preceding pages to find the words you need. You may have to make several starts before you get a chain of the length you want. When you are satisfied, copy your chain here.

con cur

EXTRA PRACTICE A, AN—DIS, DI, DIF

EXERCISE 1 Fill in the root and its meaning for each word. Some roots are used more than once.

WORD	ROOT	MEANING
1. prognosticate	_____	_____
2. ambiguity	_____	_____
3. autocrat	_____	_____
4. biology	_____	_____
5. circumvent	_____	_____
6. credible	_____	_____
7. demographic	_____	_____
8. disparity	_____	_____
9. antagonize	_____	_____
10. synchronize	_____	_____
11. collusion	_____	_____
12. precursor	_____	_____
13. jurisdiction	_____	_____
14. discordant	_____	_____
15. millennium	_____	_____
16. anterior	_____	_____
17. anthropology	_____	_____
18. antithesis	_____	_____
19. benign	_____	_____
20. bisect	_____	_____
21. chronicle	_____	_____
22. anticipate	_____	_____
23. exceed	_____	_____
24. cursory	_____	_____
25. anomaly	_____	_____

QUIZ YOURSELF Visit the student companion website at www.cengagebrain.com to check your progress by working with the audio flashcards.

21 EQU—equal

If you're looking for a climate that's *equally* pleasant in summer and winter, you're looking for an **equable** climate. If you're eager for spring, you're waiting for the spring **equinox**, when days and nights are *equal*. If you want a fair settlement of a legal case, you want an **equitable** settlement. And if you can remain *equally* calm and composed under pleasant or unpleasant circumstances, you're able to maintain your **equanimity**.

equable (ek´ wuh bul) adjective—equal at all times; unvarying. *Hawaii has an equable climate, equally pleasant in summer and winter.*

equanimity (e kwuh nim´ uh tē) [EQU equal + ANIM mind] noun—evenness of mind or temper; composure. *No matter what happened, she always maintained her equanimity.*

equate (i kwāt) verb—to represent as equal. *Don't equate money with happiness.*

equator (i kwat´ ur) noun—a line equally distant at all points from the North and South Poles. *The equator runs through the country Ecuador, which is how the country got its name.*

equilateral (ē kwuh lat´ ur ul) [EQU equal + LATER side] adjective—having equal sides. *He drew an equilateral triangle on the board.*

equilibrium (ē kwuh lib´ re um) [EQU equal + LIBR balance] noun—a state of balance. *When the horse swerved, the boy lost his equilibrium and fell off.*

equinox (ē ´ kwuh noks) [EQU equal + NOX night] noun—literally equal night; the time of year when the sun crosses the equator and day and night are of equal length. *Each year the vernal or spring equinox falls on March 20.*

equitable (ek´ wuh tuh bul) adjective—reasonable; fair; just. *They achieved an equitable settlement out of court.*

equity (ek´ wuh tē) noun—fair, even, just; also an ownership right to property. *The couple found equity: he cooked dinner and she did the dishes.*

equivalent (i kwiv´ u lunt) [EQU equal + VALE strength] noun—equal in value, force, or meaning. *The prize was equivalent to a month's wages.*

equivocal (i kwiv´ uh kul) [EQU equal + VOC voice] adjective—literally having equal voices; capable of two interpretations. *Her equivocal reply was so carefully worded that the members of each side thought she favored them.*

equivocate (i kwiv´ uh kāt) [EQU equal + VOC voice] verb—to make statements with two possible meanings in order to mislead. *The candidate equivocated so much that it was impossible to tell where he stood on any issue.*

inadequate (in ad´ i kwut) [AD to + EQU equal] adjective—not equal to what is required; insufficient. *My preparation for that exam was inadequate, so I did not score as high as I needed to to get the job.*

ALSO: adequate, equalize, equation, equidistant, inequality, inequity, iniquity, unequivocal

EXERCISE 1 Write the correct **EQU** word next to its definition.

equable	equanimity	equate
inadequate	equivocal	equilibrium
equitable	equity	equivocate

1. _____ to represent as equal
2. _____ reasonable, fair, just
3. _____ capable of two interpretations
4. _____ equal at all times, unvarying
5. _____ an ownership right to property
6. _____ state of balance
7. _____ statements with two possible meanings in order to mislead
8. _____ evenness of mind or temper; composure
9. _____ not equal to what is required or what is insufficient

 EXERCISE 2 Write the appropriate **EQU** word.

1. It is not always possible to _____ salary and job satisfaction.
2. Because John has so often _____ (ed), people are reluctant to believe him.
3. Having paid off the mortgage, we now have full _____ in our house.
4. My mother's _____ in times of crisis is amazing.
5. We must find an _____ between our work and our family.
6. Florida has a more _____ climate than Maine.
7. After the fall _____, the days get shorter.
8. An _____ triangle has three 60 degree angles.
9. In giving an _____ answer, she tried to please everyone but actually pleased no one.
10. An _____ agreement was finally reached by the divorcing couple.
11. The amount of lumber was _____ for the project, so we had to buy more.
12. According to the grading sheet, a score of 85 is _____ to a "B."
13. The _____ intersects South America, central Africa, and Indonesia.

22 EU—good, well

If you are in a state of **euphoria**, you feel that life is *good,* that everything is going *well.* EU always means *good* or *well.* A **eulogy** is a speech that says *good* things about someone; **euphonious** prose has a pleasant (*good*) sound; and the controversial subject of **euthanasia** is concerned literally with a *good* death, a death for merciful reasons.

Do you ever use **euphemisms**? Look under *euphemism* in the following list and find out.

eulogize (yO´ luh jiz) [EU good + LOG speech] verb—literally to give a good speech; to give a speech in praise of something or someone. *The school's superintendent eulogized the popular principal at her retirement dinner.*

eulogy (yO´ luh je) [EU good + LOG speech] noun—literally a good speech; spoken or written praise of someone or something, especially praise of a person who has recently died. *Abraham Lincoln gave a moving eulogy at the funeral of his friend and statesman Henry Clay.*

euphemism (yO´ fuh miz um) noun—the substitution of a mild (*good*) word in place of a distasteful or unpleasant one. *She spoke in euphemisms, talking of "passing on" rather than dying, of the "departed" rather than the dead, and of the "underprivileged" rather than the poor.*

euphonious (yO fo´ nē us) [EU good + PHON sound] adjective—having a pleasant (*good*) sound; harmonious. *The euphonious sounds of the forest are relaxing.*

euphony (yO´ fuh nē) [EU good + PHON sound] noun—literally good sound; a harmonious succession of words having a pleasing sound. *I like the euphony of the speeches of Martin Luther King Jr.*

euphoria (yO for´ ē uh) noun—a feeling of well-being. *After she became engaged, she was in a state of euphoria.*

euthanasia (yO thuh nā´ zhuh) [EU good + THAN death] noun—literally a good death; painless putting to death for merciful reasons, as with a terminal illness. *Belgium is one of the few countries where euthanasia is legal for those who are suffering and will not get well.*

ALSO: eucalyptus, Eucharist, Eugene, eugenics

EXERCISE 1 Write the correct EU word next to its definition.

eulogize	euphemism	euphonious
eulogy	euphoria	euthanasia

1. _____ a feeling of well-being
2. _____ having a pleasant sound
3. _____ to give a speech in praise of
4. _____ painless putting to death for merciful reasons
5. _____ substitution of a mild word in place of a distasteful one
6. _____ a spoken or written praise, especially of someone who has recently died

EXERCISE 2   Write the appropriate EU word.

1. In Oregon, _____ is legal for the terminally ill.

2. Aaron's piano playing is _____ to his teacher's ears.

3. Mark Anthony's _____ after the death of Julius Caesar is one of the best-known passages in Shakespeare's writing.

4. After earning an A+ on her report, Diane was in a state of _____.

5. The philanthropist was _____ at his funeral for his charitable work.

6. The _____ of nursery rhymes is soothing to babies.

7. Instead of speaking bluntly, she used _____ to convey her meaning.

✎ **EXERCISE 3 JOURNAL   Write several sentences in your *vocabulary journal* using words from the EQU and EU sections about something that made you feel good. Be sure the sentences show the words' meaning.**

✎ **EXERCISE 4 REVIEW   Write a C in front of each sentence in which all words are used correctly.**

1. _____ To circumvent is to open all the windows.

2. _____ History is usually taught in chronological order.

3. _____ Her explanation, full of circumlocutions, never did get to the point.

4. _____ The speaker's long discourse on dieting was boring.

5. _____ A convivial group gathered for the holiday celebration.

6. _____ My friend and I collaborated to design the poster.

7. _____ The supervisor went around to circumspect each employee's work.

8. _____ A companion was originally a person with whom one shared bread.

9. _____ The father is an autocrat; the rest of the family bows to his wishes.

10. _____ A credulous person tends to believe without sufficient evidence.

11. _____ A disproportionate amount of his salary went toward paying his rent.

12. _____ A consensus is the recording of the population in an area.

13. _____ The music teacher was pleased with the euthanasia playing of her students.

14. _____ Realizing he was outmatched, the chess player receded the game.

15. _____ My reading teacher taught us to predict the ending of the story.

23 EX, ES, E—out

Our word **escape** means breaking loose from any confinement, but originally it had a more picturesque meaning. In Roman times, perhaps when a jailor was trying to hang on to a prisoner by his cape, the prisoner slipped *out* of his cape and left it in the hands of the jailor: The prisoner had escaped (ES out + CAP cape). He had gotten "out of his cape" and gone free.

ebullient (i bOl´ yunt) [E out + BULL to bubble or boil] adjective—bubbling out; overflowing with enthusiasm. *The cheerleaders' ebullient manner got the crowd to stand and root for their team.*

efface (i fās´) [E out + FAC face] verb—to wipe out. *Nothing could efface the memory of that destructive storm.*

emigrate (em´ uh grāt) [E out + MIGRA to move] verb—to move out of a country (in contrast to immigrate, which means to move into a country). *My ancestors emigrated from Mexico to Brazil.*

emit (ē mit´) [E out + MIT to send] verb—to send out, as a child emits a scream or a factory emits smoke. *The boy emitted a yell when he touched the hot stove.*

enervate (en´ ur vāt) [E out + NERV nerve] verb—literally to take out the nerve; to deprive of nerve, force, or vigor; to weaken. *She did not want to leave her air-conditioned room; she found the hot, humid climate enervating.*

eradicate (i rad´ i kāt) [E out + RADIC root] verb—literally to tear out by the roots; to destroy. *It's difficult to eradicate all of the weeds from my large garden.*

excoriate (ek skor´ e āt) [EX out + COR skin] verb—to denounce harshly. *The candidate excoriated her opponent, lashing out at him in her public speeches.*

exonerate (eg zon´ uh rāt) [EX out + ONER burden] verb—literally to take the burden out; to free from a charge or from guilt. *The jury exonerated him from all charges.*

expatiate (ek spā shē āt) [EX out + SPATIUM space, course] verb—literally to wander out of the course; to digress; to speak or write at length. *The salesperson expatiated on the value of the product until everyone was bored.*

expatriate (eks pāt´ rē ut) [EX out + PATRIA native country] noun—one who has left one's country or renounced allegiance to it. *She was an expatriate from Germany, now living in Greece.*

export (ek sport´) [EX out + PORT to carry] verb—to carry out of a country, usually a product for sale or trade. *China exports products to countries all over the world.*

expurgate (eks´ pur gāt) [EX out + PURG to clean] verb—to take out obscene or objectionable material. *The cast voted to expurgate a violent scene from the play.*

exterminate (ek stur´ muh nāt) [EX out + TERMINUS boundary] verb—to destroy utterly and is applied to insects or people. *I'm trying to exterminate these cockroaches.*
(Exterminate and eradicate are nearly synonymous. Exterminate means to destroy utterly and is applied to insects or people. Eradicate implies an uprooting and is applied to a disease, a fault, or a prejudice.)

ALSO: edict, eject, emissary, erase, erupt, escape, evoke, exacerbate, excavate, exclaim, excise, exclude, exculpate, exodus, expedite, expel, extort

✎ **EXERCISE 1** **Write the correct EX, ES, E word next to its definition.**

emit	expatiate	enervate	ebullient	exterminate
excoriate	eradicate	export	exonerate	

1. _____ to carry out of a country
2. _____ to send out
3. _____ to destroy as in a disease, a fault, or a prejudice
4. _____ to denounce harshly
5. _____ to digress; to speak or write at length
6. _____ overflowing with enthusiasm
7. _____ to deprive of nerve, force, vigor; to weaken
8. _____ to free from charge or guilt
9. _____ to destroy utterly, applied to insects or people

✎ **EXERCISE 2** **Write the appropriate EX, ES, E word.**

1. The accused is certain the evidence will _____ him.
2. The editor will _____ the offensive language from the novel.
3. During World War II, Nazis used the euphemism "_____" for the murder of Jews.
4. With more research, AIDS may someday be _____ (ed).
5. She _____ (s) about her ailments until our eyes glaze over.
6. The angry speaker will _____ anyone who disagrees with him.
7. The kindergarten teacher's _____ personality helps the children to be excited about their learning.
8. My grandparents _____ (ed) from Ireland to the United States during the Potato Famine.
9. The smoke alarm _____ (s) a shrill whistle.
10. The English poet Lord Byron was an _____ living in Italy.
11. The bronze letters on the monument have not been _____.
12. Having the flu _____ me.

✎ **EXERCISE 3 JOURNAL** **In your *vocabulary journal*, write a few sentences describing some people you know. Use as many of your EX, ES, and E vocabulary words as possible.**

Did you ever wonder how Fido got his name? He's called Fido because he's *faithful* to his master. The root FID always has something to do with *faith*. **Fidelity** means *faith*fulness, and **infidelity** means un*faith*fulness. If you are **confident**, you have *faith* in yourself, but if you are **diffident** [DI not + FID faith], you don't have *faith* in yourself; you are shy. If you sign an **affidavit**, there is *faith* that your signature and statement are true.

Sometimes, as in **confide, confident, confidential**, CON is used merely as an intensive, giving more emphasis to the root that follows.

bona fide (bo´ nuh fīd) [BON good + FID faith] adjective—literally in good faith; genuine. *They made a bona fide offer on the house. The museum has a bona fide painting by Gauguin.*

confidant (kahn´ fuh dant) [CON (intensive) + FID faith] noun—literally a person one has faith in; a person one confides in. *Her dad has been her confidant for years.*

confide (kun fīd´) [CON (intensive) + FID faith] noun—to show faith by sharing secrets. *I confide my deepest fears and dreams to my best friend.*

confident (kahn´ fud unt) [CON (intensive) + FID faith] adjective—having faith in oneself, self-assured. *The actor was confident as he walked onto the stage.*

confidential (kahn fuh den´ chul) [CON (intensive) + FID faith] adjective—marked by intimacy or willingness to confide. *The personnel files were marked confidential.*

diffident (dif´ uh dunt) [DIF not + FID faith] adjective—not having faith in oneself; shy; timid. *Many people are diffident about speaking in public, but with practice they can overcome this.*

fidelity (fi del´ uh tē) noun—faithfulness. *His fidelity to the party platform was unquestionable.*

infidel (in´ fuh dul) [IN not + FID faith] noun—literally not faithful; a person who does not believe in a particular religion. *The devout Muslims were in conflict with the infidels.*

infidelity (in fuh del´ uh tē) [IN not + FID faith] noun—unfaithfulness, especially in marriage. *Anna divorced her husband because of his infidelity.*

perfidious (per fid´ ē us) [PER through + FID faith] adjective—deceiving through a pretense of faith; treacherous. *In the movies, a perfidious character often threatens the love interest of the main character.*

ALSO: affidavit, confidence, perfidy

✎ **EXERCISE 1   Write the appropriate FID word.**

1. He owns a _____ 1908 Model T Ford.

2. The _____ student did not join the other students in playing tag during recess.

3. His _____ attempts to undermine the work of his own committee were shocking.

4. Anyone not following the state religion was called a(n) _____.

5. You can be sure of his _____; he would never be unfaithful.

6. She needed a _____ with whom she could discuss her problems.

7. Juan and his best friend _____ in each other.

8. Most employee records are _____ because they contain personal information.

9. Alberta's constant _____ caused their marriage to end.

10. Having earned "A's" and "B's" on all her tests, Kailee was _____ she would pass the final.

✎ **EXERCISE 2   Write the appropriate FID word in the blank space.**

My best friend, Susan, is my _____. I _____

in her knowing that she will keep my thoughts _____. She is

unlike a false friend I had in the past, who was _____. I am

quiet and _____, so it is important to me that my friends show

_____.

✎ **EXERCISE 3 JOURNAL   Using the FID words you just studied, write several sentences about a faithful friend in your *vocabulary journal*.**

25 GEN—birth, race, kind

In ancient mythology, when a child was born, a guardian spirit or **genius** (so named because it appeared at *birth*) was appointed to guide the person throughout life. Today, although we no longer believe we are given a guiding genius at birth, we may still have within us from *birth* a genius for something such as math or painting. Thus the ancient guiding genius has now become an exceptional intellectual or creative ability.

GEN has four main meanings.

1. First of all, **GEN** means *birth*—not only the *birth* of people but also the *birth* of things (an engine **generates** or gives *birth* to electricity) and the *birth* of ideas (angry words **engender** or give *birth* to hate, whereas kind words engender love).

engender (in jen´ dur) [EN in + GEN birth] verb—to develop; to bring forth, as ideas or feelings. *His ability to solve complex problems engenders the respect of his colleagues.*

generate (jen´ uh rāt) verb—to produce, as an engine generates power. *By turning a windmill, the wind can generate electricity.*

generation (jen uh rā´ shun) noun—all the people born at about the same time. *Parents and grandparents usually try to understand the younger generation.*

genesis (jen´ uh sis) noun—the birth or coming into being of anything; origin; creation. *His many childhood pets were the genesis of his interest in zoology.*

genius (jen´ yus) noun—in ancient mythology, a guardian spirit appointed at birth to guide a person; now, an exceptional intellectual or creative ability. *Ludwig Van Beethoven, one of the most famous and influential composers of all time, was a musical genius.*

hydrogen (hi´ druh jun) [HYDR water + GEN birth] noun—a gas so called because it generates (gives birth to) water by its combustion. *Hydrogen gas was used in the first balloons to carry men into the sky.*

ingenious (in jen´ yus) [IN in + GEN birth] adjective—literally having inborn talent; clever, skillful, inventive. *It took an ingenious architect to design a house for such a small lot.*

ingenuous (in jen´ yO us) [IN in + GEN birth] adjective—showing innocent or childlike simplicity or gullibility; unsophisticated. *She was completely ingenuous, always credulous.*

2. **GEN** also indicates noble or good *birth* or breeding.

generous (jen´ uh rus) adjective—giving freely; liberal in giving. *Volunteers are generous in giving their time to charity organizations.*

genial (je´ ne ul) adjective—having a friendly and kindly manner. *His genial personality made him a favorite party guest.*

genteel (jen tēl´) adjective—having an aristocratic quality; refined in manner. *She was genteel and, therefore, unused to coarse manners.*

gentility (jen til´ uh tē) noun—the condition of being genteel. *We enjoyed the hospitality of Southern gentility during our vacation in Louisiana.*

gentleman (jen´ tl man) noun—originally a man of noble or gentle birth, now a polite, considerate man. *If a man is just, merciful, and kindly, he is a gentleman.*

gentry (jen´ trē) noun—people of gentle birth or high social position. *The town's gentry were its most powerful members.*

3. **GEN** also means *race*. If you are interested in your family history, you are interested in **genealogy**, the study of the ancestors of a family.

gene (jen) noun—a unit of heredity made up of molecules and cells that give living organisms their physical characteristics (DNA and RNA). *Information stored in the genes determines an individual's eye color.*

genealogy (je nē al′ uh je) [GEN race + -LOGY study of] noun—*literally the study of race;* the study of family descent. *While researching her genealogy, Sara discovered that her great-grandfather was a famous rabbi in Poland.*

genetics (juh net′ iks) noun—the science of heredity. *The Human Genome Project will allow scientists to map the genetics of most mammals.*

genocide (jen′ uh sīd) [GEN race + CID to kill] noun—the systematic, planned killing of a racial, political, or cultural group. *In Rwanda, in 1994, Hutus killed over 800,000 Tutsis in 100 days in an act of genocide.*

progenitor (pro jen′ uh tur) [PRO forth + GEN birth] noun—a direct ancestor. *Leopold Mozart, the progenitor of Wolfgang Amadeus Mozart, was also a musical genius.*

progeny (proj′ uh nē) [PRO forth + GEN birth] noun—children or descendants. *His progeny inherited his red, curly hair.*

4. **GEN** also means a category or *kind*.

generic (juh ner′ ik) adjective—general kind; commonly available; not protected by a trademark, as generic drugs. *She usually economizes by buying generic brands instead of name brands.*

genre (zhahn′ ruh) noun—a particular kind or category of literature, art, music, film, theater. *He hadn't limited his reading to a single genre but had delved into poetry, the short story, and the novel.*

Also: congenital, degenerate, eugenics, general, heterogeneous, homogeneous, homogenize, pathogenic, primogeniture

EXERCISE 1   Write the appropriate GEN word.

1. Rodney _____(s) ideas for his essays easily.

2. Her _____ behavior made her welcome wherever she went.

3. Our _____ determine most of our physical features.

4. Many prescription plans require patients to use _____ medications if available.

5. My favorite musical _____ is jazz.

6. The _____ of most ideas begins with creative thought.

7. _____ always treat ladies with respect.

8. The manager's rude behavior did not _____ respect from her workers.

9. On Father's Day, George's _____ filled his house.

10. His _____ design won his company the contract.

11. She traced her _____ to six countries on three different continents.

12. _____ is unacceptable in any civilized society.

EXERCISE 2   Circle the GEN word that is used correctly in each sentence.

1. The Stein family, whose (progenitors, genetics) emigrated from Spain early in the nineteenth century, settled in Atlanta.

2. His father's dominant (genealogy, genes) were passed on to all his children.

3. The (genial, ingenuous) doctor had a great bedside manner, especially when it came to her older patients.

4. (Hydrogen, Gentility) is used in vegetable oils to make margarines and spreads.

5. My (gentry, generous) nature prevents me from refusing any beggar who approaches me.

6. Former newscaster and author Tom Brokaw named the people who lived through the Great Depression and World War II the "Greatest (Generation, Genre)" for all they sacrificed for their country.

7. The young man was simple-minded and (generic, ingenuous).

 EXERCISE 3   Write a sentence of your own for each GEN word.

1. engender _____

_____

_____

2. genetics _____

_____

_____

3. genocide _____

_____

_____

4. progeny _____

_____

_____

5. generic _____

_____

_____

6. genesis _____

_____

_____

EXTRA PRACTICE A, AN—GEN

EXERCISE 1 Write C in front of each sentence in which the underlined word is used correctly. If it is used incorrectly, write X in front of the sentence.

1. _____ The internet makes it easy to <u>disseminate</u> information quickly.
2. _____ Her excuse was so <u>credible</u> that no one believed her.
3. _____ It usually is possible to <u>correlate</u> vocabulary and success in college.
4. _____ They had a <u>symbiotic</u> relationship, each working better when they worked together.
5. _____ The judge's lenient sentence set a <u>precedent;</u> never had a robber been sentenced to only community service.
6. _____ A <u>cursory</u> is an error in a term paper.
7. _____ A <u>bilateral</u> agreement is written in two languages.
8. _____ <u>Coherent</u> writing is orderly and easy to follow.
9. _____ A <u>genetic</u> animal can live both on land and in water.
10. _____ The <u>autocrat</u> followed democratic principles.

EXERCISE 2 Fill in the root and its meaning for each word.

WORD	ROOT	MEANING
1. prognosticate	_____	_____
2. per annum	_____	_____
3. cursory	_____	_____
4. antidote	_____	_____
5. curriculum	_____	_____
6. diction	_____	_____
7. autonomy	_____	_____
8. benevolence	_____	_____
9. anti meridiem	_____	_____
10. anthropomorphic	_____	_____
11. amoral	_____	_____
12. circumspect	_____	_____
13. biopsy	_____	_____
14. chronic	_____	_____
15. ambivalence	_____	_____

QUIZ YOURSELF Visit the student companion website at www.cengagebrain.com to check your progress by working with the audio flashcards.

26 GRAPH, GRAM—to write

We don't usually think of **geography** as having anything to do with writing, but it is made up of GEO, *earth,* and GRAPH, to *write,* and is actually a *writing* about the surface of the Earth. Note how each of the following words has something to do with *writing.*

calligraphy (kuh lig´ ruh fē) [CALLI beautiful + GRAPH to write] noun—the art of fine handwriting. *In beautiful calligraphy, she copied her favorite poem and had it framed.*

cardiogram (kahr´ de uh gram) [CARD heart + GRAM to write] noun—a written tracing showing the contractions of the heart. *The cardiogram showed a few extra heartbeats.*

choreography (kor e og´ ruh fē) [CHOR dance + GRAPH to write] noun—literally the writing of a story in dance; the creating and arranging of dance movements. *Alvin Ailey was known for his ingenious choreography.*

diagram (di´ uh gram) [DIA by, through + GRAPH to write] noun—a drawing that shows how something works, appears or is structured. *The diagram shows the circulatory system of the human body.*

epigram (ep´ uh gram) [EPI on + GRAM to write] noun—any short, witty saying. *She liked to quote the epigram "Success is getting what you want; happiness is wanting what you get."*

geography (je og´ ruh fē) [GEO earth + GRAPH to write] noun—literally a writing about the Earth; a science dealing with the Earth and its life. *The study of geography helps us better understand climate change.*

graffiti (gra fe´ tē) noun—crude drawings or writings scratched on public walls. *Expurgating objectionable graffiti on the subway walls was the next civic project.*

graphic (graf´ ik) adjective—full of vivid details. *The movie's graphic description of the earthquake scared some of the audience.*

hologram (ho´ luh gram) [HOLO whole + GRAM to write] noun—a three-dimensional photograph made using lasers. *The cover of the* National Geographic *for December 1988 was a hologram.*

monograph (mon´ uh graf) [MONO one + GRAPH to write] noun—a book written about one specific subject. *She published a monograph about the biblical references in Robert Browning's poems.*

seismograph (sīz´ muh graf) [SEISMOS earthquake + GRAPH to write] noun—an instrument for recording (writing) the intensity and duration of an earthquake. *The seismograph recorded an earthquake that registered 7 on the Richter scale.*

topography (tuh pahg´ ruh fē) [TOP place + GRAPH to write] noun—a detailed drawing (writing) on a map of the surface features of a region (place) showing their relative positions and elevations. *Before venturing into the canyon, the hikers studied its topography.*

ALSO: autobiography, autograph, bibliography, biography, cryptography, demographic, graphite, lithography, monogram, orthography, phonograph, photography, program, stenographer, telegram, telegraph

✎ EXERCISE 1   Write the appropriate GRAPH, GRAM word.

1. His fiancée hired me to write the wedding invitations in _____.

2. The library catalogs all published _____ (s), including the latest, *The History of Perfume.*

3. His _____ showed the need for further medical tests.

4. If you look at a _____ from different angles, it looks just as if you were looking at the real object.

5. A study of the _____ of the region showed many valleys and hills.

6. The fence around the construction was covered with amusing _____.

7. Children shouldn't watch movies with _____ violence or adult themes.

8. The flowing motion of the _____ captured the theme of the dance.

9. The _____ showed the circuits within the computer.

10. The _____ recorded fifteen small earthquakes in a twenty-four-hour period.

11. One of Oscar Wilde's frequently quoted _____ (s) is "I can resist everything except temptation."

12. The _____ of Maine is diverse.

✎ EXERCISE 2   Write C in front of each sentence in which the GRAM, GRAPH word is used correctly. Then, in each remaining blank, write the word that should have been used.

1. _____ Mark Twain wrote one of my favorite epigrams: "Man is the only animal that blushes. Or needs to."

2. _____ The earthquake measured 8.5 according to the monograph reading.

3. _____ For their senior project, students drew the topography of the trail.

4. _____ Some of Brazil's physical geography is uncharted because it is inaccessible to humans.

5. _____ The dance company's calligraphy used arrangements never seen before.

✎ EXERCISE 3 JOURNAL   Using the GRAPH, GRAM words you just studied, write several sentences about writing you have done for school or pleasure in your *vocabulary journal.*

27 | HYPER—overmuch, too far

Do you know someone who exaggerates? He or she is using **hyperbole**, a figure of speech that uses embellishment and comes from the roots HYPER, meaning *too far* and BAINEIN, meaning *to step*. You've probably heard such expressions as "I've tried to diet a thousand times" or "Your suitcase weighs a ton!" These exaggerations are used to emphasize a point and are not meant to be taken literally.

hyperactive (hy per ac´ tiv) [HYPER overmuch + ACTUS a doing] adjective—more active than is usual or desirable. *His hyperactive mind allowed him to think about several things at once.*

hyperbaton (hy per bah´ tun) [HYPER overmuch + BAINEIN to step] noun—literally overstepping; a rhetorical device using inverted word order to produce an effect. *Yoda speaks in hyperbaton, for example, "Ready are you? What know you of ready?"*

hyperbole (hy per´ bō lē) [HYPER overmuch + BOL to throw] noun—a figure of speech in which exaggeration is used for emphasis or effect. *Her hyperbole caused the audience to laugh.*

hypercritical (hy per crīt i´ cal) [HYPER overmuch + KRITIKE the art of judgment] adjective—extremely or unreasonably critical. *My art teacher's hypercritical comments about my painting blocked my creativity.*

hyperglycemia (hy per glīcē´ mē uh) [HYPER overmuch + GLYCEMIA presence of glucose in the blood] noun—excess sugar in the blood. *Signs of hyperglycemia are thirst, a dry mouth, and a need to urinate.*

hyperopic (hy per o´ pik) [HYPER overmuch + OPTOS seen, visible] noun—condition of the eye in which vision is better for distant objects than for near objects; farsightedness. *After being diagnosed hyperopic, he was fitted with glasses.*

hypertension (hy per ten´ shun) [HYPER overmuch + TENDERE to stretch] noun— abnormally high blood pressure. *People with hypertension are at risk for heart disease.*

hypertrophy (hy per´ trō fē) [HYPER overmuch + TROPHY food, nourishment] noun— exaggerated growth. *His extensive weight lifting led to hypertrophy of his biceps.*

ALSO: hyperactivity, hyperextend, hyperinflation, hypersonic, hyperthermia, hyperventilate

✎ **EXERCISE 1**   **Match the HYPER word to its definition.**

1. _____ hyperactive
2. _____ hyperbaton
3. _____ hyperopic
4. _____ hyperbole
5. _____ hypertension
6. _____ hypertrophy
7. _____ hyperglycemia
8. _____ hypercritical

A. abnormally high blood pressure

B. exaggerated growth

C. more active than is usual or desirable

D. farsightedness

E. extremely critical

F. figure of speech in which exaggeration is used for emphasis or effect

G. excess sugar in the blood

H. a figure of speech using inverted word order

✎ **EXERCISE 2**   **Write the correct HYPER word.**

1. Nothing can satisfy that _____ customer.

2. Some of the best authors of tall tales use _____ to add humor to their stories.

3. My eye doctor offered information about the causes of my _____ vision.

4. Using steroids can lead to muscle _____.

5. Shakespeare uses _____ when he has King Henry IV say, "Uneasy lies the head that wears the crown."

6. Dave's doctor was concerned about his _____, fearing it may affect his heart.

7. A common cause of chronic _____ is overeating carbohydrates and sugar.

8. The _____ child who ran from activity to activity exhausted her mother.

✎ **EXERCISE 3 JOURNAL**   **Write several sentences in your *vocabulary journal* about someone or something that shows the meaning of the root HYPER.**

28 LOG—speech, word

Words containing the root LOG have to do with *speech*. A **monologue** [MONO one + LOG speech] is a *speech* by one person. A **dialogue** [DIA between + LOG speech] is a *speech* between two or more people. A **prologue** [PRO before + LOG speech] is a *speech* before a play, and an **epilogue** [EPI upon + LOG speech] is a *speech* after it. (Note that all of these words can also be spelled without the *ue* ending.)

analogous (uh nal' uh gus) [ANA according to + LOG speech, reason] adjective—similar in some ways but not in others. *The wings of a bird and those of an airplane are analogous, having a similar function but a different origin and structure.*

analogy (uh nal' uh je) [ANA according to + LOG speech, reason] noun—resemblance in some particulars between things otherwise unlike. *To get his point across, the professor used the following analogy: Cutting classes is like paying for a hamburger and then walking away without eating it.*

apology (uh pul' uh je) [AB away from + LOG speech] noun—literally a speech in defense; an expression of regret asking forgiveness for a fault or an offense. *I accepted her sincere apology for saying unkind things about me.*

dialogue (di' uh log) [DIA between + LOG speech] noun—speech between two or more people; a conversational passage in a play or narrative. *After a long dialogue, we finally resolved our difficulties.*

epilogue (ep' uh log) [EPI on + LOG speech] noun—a speech directed to the audience at the conclusion of a literary work. *Some films, such as the last Harry Potter movie, end with an epilogue that explains what happens to the characters in the future.*

monologue (mon' uh log) [MONO one + LOG speech] noun—a speech by one person; a soliloquy. *The school's superintendent gave an impassioned monologue about the need for a new school in the town.*

prologue (pro' log) [PRO before + LOG speech] noun—a speech before a play. Romeo and Juliet *begins with a prologue that summarizes the story for the audience.* Also, any introductory event. *The fancy appetizers were the prologue to an excellent dinner.*

ALSO: analog, Decalogue, doxology, eulogy, logic, travelogue

✎ **EXERCISE 1   Match each LOG word with its definition.**

1. _____ apology   **A.** an expression of regret asking forgiveness for a fault or an offense
2. _____ analogy   **B.** a speech before a play
3. _____ epilogue   **C.** a speech between two or more people
4. _____ prologue   **D.** resemblance in some ways between things otherwise unlike
5. _____ dialogue   **E.** a speech directed to the audience at the end of a play
6. _____ analogous   **F.** a speech by one person
7. _____ monologue   **G.** similar in some ways but not in others

✎ **EXERCISE 2   Write the appropriate LOG word.**

1. Studying a(n) _____ is important when making comparisons.
2. In *The Lord of the Rings*, Sam and Bilbo have a spirited _____ about the Golem.
3. Her first complaint was just a _____ of what was to come.
4. Alone on stage, Richard III starts his famous _____ with "Now is the winter of our discontent, Made glorious summer by this son of York."
5. Reading a book is _____ to dropping chemicals into a test tube: There should be a reaction.
6. An _____ was issued by the transit department to their customers for posting the incorrect train schedule.
7. Shakespeare used an _____ to end his play *A Midsummer Night's Dream*.

✎ **EXERCISE 3 WORD LIST   Remember to add words to your WORD LIST after each session. Adding just a word or two each session as well as using a few of these words in conversation each day will help you to increase your vocabulary.**

29   -LOGY—study of

-LOGY at the end of a word usually means *study of*. **Biology** [BIO life] is the *study of* plant and animal life. **Geology** [GEO earth] is the *study of* the history of the Earth, especially as recorded in rocks. **Etymology** [ETYM true] is the *study of* the origin (true meaning) and development of words. In this book, you are getting an introduction to etymology.

Almost all such words have O in front of the -LOGY so that the ending is -OLOGY. But two words have A in front of the -LOGY—**genealogy** and **mineralogy**.

anthropology (an thruh pol' uh je) [ANTHROP human + -LOGY study of] noun—a study of the physical, social, and cultural development and behavior of human beings. *Shanna studied the anthropology of Australia's Aboriginal society.*

archeology (ahr ke ol' uh je) [ARCH ancient + -LOGY study of] noun—the study of ancient cultures based on artifacts and other remains. *Egypt is a good place to study archeology because the monuments and artifacts are well preserved.*

ecology (e kol' uh je) [ECO home + -LOGY study of] noun—the study of the relationship between organisms and their environment (home). *The ecology of the region showed that the number of wild animals had decreased as a result of lumbering.*

entomology (en tuh mol' uh je) [EN in + TOM to cut + -LOGY study of] noun—the study of insects (whose bodies are "cut" in three segments). *The entomology class was studying grasshoppers.*

etymology (et uh mol' uh je) [ETYM true + -LOGY study of] noun—the study of the origin (true meaning) and development of words. *From his study of etymology, he learned many interesting word histories.*

geology (je ol' uh je) [GEO earth + -LOGY study of] noun—the study of the history of the Earth, especially as recorded in rocks. *The geology of the Grand Canyon shows various periods in the Earth's development.*

meteorology (me te uh rol' uh je) [METEORA things in the air + -LOGY study of] noun—the study of the atmosphere, especially weather and weather conditions. *The Bureau of Meteorology is recording slight changes in climate from year to year.*

ornithology (awr nuh thol' uh je) [ORNITH bird + -LOGY study of] noun—the branch of zoology dealing with birds. *Because he was interested in ornithology, he made recordings of bird songs.*

psychology (si kol' uh je) [PSYCH mind + -LOGY study of] noun—the study of mental processes and behavior. *His study of psychology helped him understand himself.*

theology (thee ahl' uh je) [THEO god + -LOGY study of] noun—the study of God and religion. *Fascinated by religion's effect on the world, he majored in theology.*

ALSO: astrology, bacteriology, biology, chronology, dermatology, embryology, genealogy, gynecology, mineralogy, morphology, paleontology, pathology, physiology, technology, zoology

✎ **EXERCISE 1   What science makes a study of the following? Write the appropriate -LOGY word.**

1. _____ the human mind
2. _____ weather conditions
3. _____ the origin and development of words
4. _____ the history of the Earth as recorded in rocks
5. _____ ancient cultures based on their artifacts and monuments
6. _____ insects
7. _____ birds
8. _____ the study of God and religion
9. _____ the relationship of organisms to their environment
10. _____ physical, social, and cultural development and behavior of human beings

✎ **EXERCISE 2   Fill in the correct -LOGY word.**

1. Forensic _____ applies insect evidence to criminal investigations.
2. _____ predicts weather forecasts on the course of the natural world.
3. In her _____ course, she studied Judaism, Christianity, Islam, and Hinduism.
4. Because _____ is study of the physical, social, and cultural development and behavior of human beings, it answers the question "What are we?"
5. When you study word roots, you are studying _____

✎ **EXERCISE 3   Write a sentence of your own for each -LOGY word.**

1. entomology _____

_____

_____

2. archeology _____

_____

_____

3. ornithology _____

_____

_____

4. etymology _____

_____

_____

5. ecology _____

_____

_____

30 LOQU, LOC—to speak

A **soliloquy** [SOL alone + LOQU to speak] is a *speech* given by an actor, alone on the stage, to reveal private thoughts and emotions. The most famous soliloquy, of course, is Hamlet's "To be or not to be," when Hamlet reveals his feelings to the audience. Another soliloquy, this one from the Shakespearean play *Romeo and Juliet*, is Romeo's speech upon seeing Juliet, "But soft! What light through yonder window breaks? It is the East, and Juliet is the sun!"

colloquial (kuh lo´ kwe ul) [COL together + LOQU to speak] adjective—language used when people speak together informally; informal or conversational; *"Whatever" is a colloquial expression for "I don't care."*

colloquium (kuh lo´ kwe um) [COL together + LOQU to speak] noun—literally a speaking together; an academic seminar on some field of study led by several experts. *The students attended the colloquium on international relations.*

eloquent (el´ uh kwunt) [E out + LOQU to speak] adjective—fluent; persuasive. *President John F. Kennedy was known as an eloquent speaker.*

grandiloquent (gran dil´ uh kwunt) [GRAND grand + LOQU to speak] adjective—marked by a lofty, extravagantly colorful style. *In The Adventures of Huckleberry Finn, the Duke tries to trick the townspeople with his grandiloquent speech.*

loquacious (lo kwa´ shus) adjective—talkative. *Because of my loquacious coworker, I got hardly any work done today.*

soliloquy (suh lil´ uh kwe) [SOL alone + LOQU to speak] noun—a speaking alone to oneself, as in a drama. *Even if there is another character onstage, the character speaking the soliloquy thinks that he or she is alone.*

ventriloquist (ven tril´ uh kwist) [VENTR stomach + LOQU to speak] noun—literally one who speaks from the stomach; one who speaks so that the sounds seem to come from somewhere other than the speaker's mouth. *The ventriloquist mesmerized the children who thought the puppet was talking.*

ALSO: circumlocution, colloquy, elocution, eloquence, interlocutor, loquacity, obloquy

✎ **EXERCISE 1**   **Match the LOQU, LOC word with its definition.**

1. _____ loquacious
2. _____ ventriloquist
3. _____ soliloquy
4. _____ grandiloquent
5. _____ colloquial
6. _____ colloquium
7. _____ eloquent

A. speaking alone to oneself as in a drama
B. marked by lofty, extravagantly colorful style
C. language used when people speak together informally
D. an academic seminar on some field of study led by several experts
E. fluent; persuasive
F. talkative
G. one who speaks so that the sounds seem to come from somewhere other than the speaker's mouth

✎ **EXERCISE 2**   **Write the appropriate LOQU, LOC word.**

1. She was so _____ that no one else had a chance to say anything.

2. Most song lyrics are _____ rather than formal.

3. The politician hoped his _____ style of speaking, with its big words and impressive gestures, would make up for his lack of ideas.

4. A dramatist reveals a character's thoughts to the audience through a(n) _____.

5. The _____ practiced speaking without moving his lips in order to improve his performance.

6. Sixty ecology professors took part in the _____ on recycling hazardous waste.

7. The audience responded with a standing ovation to his _____ speech.

✎ **EXERCISE 3 JOURNAL**   **Write three sentences in your *vocabulary journal* about the way your teachers, friends, and family talk using many of the LOQU, LOC words you have learned. Check the sentence given in the explanation of each word to make sure you are using the word correctly.**

EXTRA PRACTICE A, AN—LOQU, LOC

EXERCISE 1 Write C in front of each sentence in which the underlined vocabulary words are used correctly.

1. _____ Cathode ray tubes in televisions are the <u>precursor</u> of digital cable television.
2. _____ Jerry did a great job of maintaining his <u>equanimity</u>, right up until he fell into the orchestra pit.
3. _____ The suit for divorce accused him of <u>gentility</u>.
4. _____ The heartless old general felt no <u>compunction</u> about sending young men into battle.
5. _____ <u>Meteorology</u> has now made weather prediction more accurate.
6. _____ Always interested in butterflies, she decided to major in <u>entomology</u>.
7. _____ The photograph made a beautiful <u>epigram</u>.
8. _____ The <u>disconsolate</u> widow spent the afternoon drinking champagne and dancing with her friends.
9. _____ Not knowing a word of French, the traveler found herself without a single <u>confidant</u> to whom to tell her troubles.
10. _____ Through the study of <u>genetics</u>, scientists are making discoveries about <u>geology</u>.
11. _____ The rock band's latest CD is a <u>bona fide</u> hit.
12. _____ My mother's secret was using several <u>diffident</u> apples in her pies.
13. _____ Parents who are <u>hypercritical</u> may discourage their children from trying new activities.
14. _____ In order to <u>recede</u>, you have to give all your attention to your task.
15. _____ I like to read the <u>dictionary</u> because I learn what words mean as well as how to pronounce them.
16. _____ The minister gave an <u>eloquent</u> sermon last Sunday.
17. _____ The term "laid to rest" is a <u>euphemism</u> for "buried."
18. _____ <u>Cognition</u> is the ability to speak in several languages.
19. _____ The prepared student was <u>confident</u> he would do well on the examination.
20. _____ Even in ancient times, the older <u>generation</u> complained about the younger one.
21. _____ My grandmother rides a motorcycle; she is an <u>anomaly</u> among her friends.
22. _____ The soft lighting and music gave a peaceful <u>ambiance</u> to the spa.
23. _____ My favorite store is holding its <u>annual</u> sale next week.
24. _____ Having a daily plan is <u>equinox</u> for students.
25. _____ Because it is a holiday weekend, we <u>anticipate</u> a lot of traffic on the highway.

EXERCISE 2 Give the meaning of each root and a word in which it is found.

ROOT	MEANING	WORD
1. A, AN		
2. AMBI, AMPHI		
3. ANN, ENN		
4. ANTE, ANTI		
5. ANTHROP		
6. ANTI		
7. AUTO		
8. BENE		
9. BI		
10. BIO		
11. CEDE, CEED		
12. CHRON		
13. CIRCUM		
14. COGNI, GNOS		
15. COM, CON, COL, COR		
16. CRED		
17. CUR		
18. DEM		
19. DICT		
20. DIS, DI, DIF		
21. EQU		
22. EU		
23. EX, ES, E		
24. FID		
25. GEN		
26. GRAPH, GRAM		
27. HYPER		
28 LOG		
29. LOGY		
30. LOQU, LOC		

EXERCISE 3 Using eight of the following nine words, fill in the blanks in the paragraph so that it makes sense. Reread the paragraph and see how satisfying it is to read a paragraph in which you are sure of all the words.

ambiguous	contradict	consensus
anticlimax	democracy	engender
grandiloquent	perennial	eulogize

Our political conventions are a graphic example of _____ at work. Before the

convention, the committee platform must reach a _____ on a platform that will

be enough to avoid offending anyone, yet strong enough to _____ support.

At the convention itself, _____ speeches _____

the candidates and _____ the opposition. Finally, although the actual

choice of a candidate is often an _____ because the outcome has been known

all along, the convention does answer the _____ human question,

"Who shall lead?"

EXERCISE 4 Underline the appropriate word.

1. He spent a (disproportionate, diverse) amount of time on the first part of the book.
2. The students were bored as the professor (expatiated, equivocated) about his pet theory.
3. Instead of reading my report carefully, the supervisor gave it only a (dictatorial, cursory) glance.
4. I couldn't get a word in with that (loquacious, colloquial) man.
5. She felt (disconcerted, enervated) by the confusing geometry problem in her trigonometry course.
6. Gorillas, chimps, and apes are considered (anthropomorphic, anthropoids).
7. The (confident, diffident) teenager spent most of his time sitting by himself at the party.
8. After working all day in the garden, I finally (eradicated, excavated) all the poison ivy.
9. After the spring (equanimity, equinox), the sun continues to follow a high path through the sky, with the days growing longer and longer.
10. The (disparity, discordant) between the bride's and groom's ages surprised many of their guests.

EXERCISE 5 Give the root that is used in each underlined word.

1. _____ The movie star tried to <u>circumvent</u> the media from filming her private time with her family.

2. _____ Clouds are studied in <u>meteorology</u>.

3. _____ In Shakespearean plays, one actor often speaks a <u>soliloquy</u> directly to the audience with no other actors on the stage.

4. _____ In the story of Aladdin, the <u>infidels</u> fence with the palace guards.

5. _____ Damon didn't like to be told the <u>malfeasance</u> of his job.

6. _____ The study of <u>anthropology</u> bridges cultural gaps.

7. _____ The exchange of $24 in beads for Manhattan Island was not <u>equitable</u>.

8. _____ The <u>demographers</u> collected data from the census.

9. _____ A <u>colloquium</u> was held to discuss the diseases now found in developing nations.

10. _____ The college <u>curriculum</u> included the study of a lab science.

QUIZ YOURSELF   Visit the student companion website at www.cengagebrain.com to check your progress by working with the audio flashcards.

31 MAL—bad

In the medieval calendar, two days in each month were marked as *dies mali* (evil days)—January 1 and 25, February 4 and 26, March 1 and 28, April 10 and 20, May 3 and 25, June 10 and 16, July 13 and 22, August 1 and 30, September 3 and 21, October 3 and 22, November 5 and 28, and December 7 and 22. Any enterprise begun on one of these *bad days* was certain to end in failure. Our word **dismal** comes from *dies mali*, but today a dismal day is merely gloomy or depressing.

Was he really ill when he stayed at home from work during the week of the World Series, or was he just malingering? **Malinger** originally meant to be in *bad* health, but, as with many words, it has changed over the years and now means to pretend to be ill to avoid duty or work.

A number of words beginning with MAL are easy to understand because MAL simply gives the word a "bad" meaning.

> malnutrition means bad nutrition
> maltreated means badly treated
> maladjusted means badly adjusted to the circumstances of one's life
> malfunction means to function badly, as an engine malfunctions
> malpractice means improper treatment of a patient by a physician

maladroit (mal uh droit´) adjective—not skillful; awkward; clumsy. *The new supervisor was maladroit in dealing with the employees.*

malady (mal´ uh dē) noun—literally a bad condition; a disease. *Science has reduced the number of incurable maladies.*

malaise (mal az´) [MAL bad + AISE ease] noun—an overall feeling of illness or depression. *As she was preparing for the interview, a slight malaise came over her.*

malcontent (mal´ kun tent) noun—one who is badly dissatisfied; a discontented or rebellious person. *He was a born malcontent, always complaining.*

malediction (mal uh dik´ shun) [MAL bad + DICT to speak] noun—a curse (opposite of benediction). *The leader of the cult pronounced a malediction upon all who did not follow him.*

malevolent (muh lev´ uh lunt) [MAL bad + VOL to wish] adjective—wishing evil toward others. *The researcher in the lab cast a malevolent glance toward the director after his data was rejected.*

malfeasance (mal fē zuns) [MAL bad + FAC to do] noun—wrongdoing, especially by a public official. *The mayor was accused of malfeasance in his distribution of public funds.*

malice (mal´ is) noun—active bad feeling or ill will. *The past president felt no malice toward the candidate who defeated him.*

malicious (muh lish´ us) adjective—intentionally bad or harmful. *It is beneficial to refuse to listen to malicious gossip.*

malign (muh line´) verb—to speak evil of; to slander. *That politician is known to malign anyone who disagrees with him.*

malignant (muh lig´ nunt) adjective—bad or harmful; likely to cause death. *The biopsy revealed that the growth was not malignant.*

malinger (muh ling´ gur) verb—to pretend to be in bad health to get out of work. *He always malingers just before school starts.*

ALSO: malapropism, malaria, malefactor, malformed, malocclusion, malodorous

✏️ **EXERCISE 1** **Write the word for each definition.**

1. _____ wishing evil toward others
2. _____ not adroit, not skillful
3. _____ bad, harmful, likely to cause death
4. _____ disease
5. _____ vague feeling of depression, ennui
6. _____ to pretend to be in bad health to get out of work
7. _____ a curse
8. _____ to speak evil of; to slander

✏️ **EXERCISE 2** **Write the appropriate MAL word.**

1. The doctor announced that the patient's _____ was chronic.
2. Even though the school conditions were ideal, the _____ always found something to complain about.
3. The doctor found a _____ tumor in her patient's liver.
4. I heard that the senator will _____ his opponent, claiming she is taking bribes.
5. Teenagers often spread _____ rumors about each other.
6. When I woke up this morning, I felt a general _____ even before I remembered the sad events of the weekend.
7. When the kickbacks were discovered, the city's commissioner was accused of _____.
8. According to the Bible, Moses laid a _____ on the Egyptians, leading to the ten plagues.
9. The insurance investigator warned the man not to _____ or he would lose his disability payments.
10. In earlier centuries, teachers forced all students to write right-handed; left-handed students were considered _____.
11. The enemy turned his _____ gaze on his foe.
12. The townspeople felt _____ toward the company that polluted their river.

32 METER, METR—measure

The **metric system** is a decimalized system of measurement first adopted by France in 1791 and now used internationally. Although for years Americans have used the root METER in such words as **thermometer**, **barometer**, **speedometer**, and **odometer**, the United States is one of the few countries in the world who have not adopted the **metric system**. Only two other countries in the world don't use metric: Liberia and Burma.

barometer (bu rahm´ uh tur) [BAR pressure + METER measure] noun—an instrument for measuring atmospheric pressure and hence for assisting in predicting probable weather changes. *The barometer reading indicates falling air pressure, which predicts rain.*

geometry (je ahm´ uh trē) [GEO earth + METR measure] noun—originally, the system of measuring distances on Earth through the use of angles; now, a branch of mathematics that deals with points, lines, planes, and solids. *I used my skill in geometry to find the angles of the polygon.*

kilometer (kuh lom´ uh tur) [KILO thousand + METER measure] noun—1,000 meters; approximately 0.62 miles. *In Canada, the speed limits are posted in kilometers.*

metric system (me´ trik) noun—a decimal system of weights and measures based on the meter as a unit length and the kilogram as a unit mass. *The metric system is used by scientists worldwide.*

metronome (met ruh nōm) [METR measure + NOM law] noun—a clocklike instrument for measuring the exact time (law) in music by a regularly repeated tick. *Practicing the piano with a metronome helped her keep perfect time.*

parameter (puh ram´ uh tar) [PARA beside + METER measure] noun—a fixed limit or boundary. *Stay within the parameters of the present budget.*

perimeter (puh rim´ uh tur) [PERI around + METER measure] noun—the boundary around an area. *An old rail fence ran along the perimeter of his farm.*

symmetrical (si met´ ri kul) [SYM together + METR measure] adjective—having both sides exactly alike. *He made symmetrical flower arrangements for both ends of the table.*

trigonometry (trig uh nom´ uh trē) [TRI three + GON angle + METR measure] noun—the branch of mathematics that deals with the relations between the sides and angles of triangles and the calculations based on these. *Her knowledge of trigonometry definitely helped her obtain a job as a land surveyor.*

ALSO: asymmetrical, centimeter, chronometer, diameter, isometric, micrometer, odometer, pedometer, pentameter, tachometer, telemetry, thermometer

EXERCISE 1 Which **METER** or **METR** word names or describes the following?

1. _____ the boundary around an area

2. _____ an instrument that measures atmospheric pressure

3. _____ a decimal system based on the meter as a unit of length and the kilogram as the unit of mass

4. _____ approximately 0.62 miles

5. _____ a branch of mathematics that deals with relations between sides and angles of triangles and their calculations

6. _____ having both sides exactly alike

7. _____ a fixed limit or boundary

8. _____ Earth measuring; now a branch of mathematics that deals with points, lines, planes, and solids

9. _____ an instrument that measures time in music by a regularly repeated tick

EXERCISE 2 REVIEW As a review of some of the roots you have learned, try to make a root chain similar to the one on pages 1–3. Start with *disconsolate*, and refer to the preceding pages to find the words you need. You may have to make several starts before you get a chain of the length you want.

dis con so late

EXERCISE 3 WORD LIST Add a few more words to your **WORD LIST**. Record words that you have heard in your classes and in conversation or that you have read in newspapers or on the Internet.

33 MIT, MIS, MISS—to send

The MIT, MIS, MISS root has to do with sending. A **mission** is a task that one is *sent* to do. A **missionary** is someone *sent* out to do religious work. A **message** is a communication *sent* to someone, and the person who carries the message is a **messenger**.

commit (kuh mit´) [Com together, with + MIT to send] verb—to pledge or bind in obligation. *The Navy Seals commit to protect and serve the United States of America.*

intermittent (in tur mit´ unt) [INTER between + MIT to send] adjective—stopping and starting at intervals. *The intermittent rain didn't prevent them from enjoying the game.*

missive (mis´ iv) noun—a letter or message that is sent. *A missive from the president directed their next move.*

omit (ō mit´) [OB away + MIT to send] verb—literally to send away; to leave out. *You'd better omit that unnecessary paragraph.*

premise (prem´ is) [PRE before + MIS to send] noun—literally a statement sent before; an initial statement that is assumed to be true and upon which an argument is based. *His argument failed because he started with a false premise.*

remiss (ri mis´) [RE back + MISS to send] adjective—literally to send back; negligent; lax in attending to duty. *I've been remiss about doing my exercises.*

remission (ri mish´ un) [RE back + MISS to send] noun—literally a sending back; a lessening, as a remission of disease; forgiveness, as a remission of sins. *He enjoyed periods of remission from his illness.*

transmit (trans mit´) [TRANS across + MIT to send] verb—to send (across) from one place or person to another. *The lawyer will transmit the document to his client.*

ALSO: admit, commission, commitment, committee, dismiss, demise, emissary, emit, intermission, omission, permit, promise, remit, submit, transmission

✏️ **EXERCISE 1 Which MIT, MIS, MISS word names or describes the following?**

1. _____ stopping and starting at intervals
2. _____ to send across
3. _____ a letter or message that is sent
4. _____ a statement assumed to be true upon which an argument is based
5. _____ negligent
6. _____ a lessening
7. _____ to leave out

✏️ **EXERCISE 2 Write the appropriate MIT, MIS, MISS word.**

1. She had a few weeks of good health during a _____ of her illness.
2. Students often _____ vital supporting details in their essays.
3. Good college students _____ to studying the etymology of words.
4. A valid argument must have a logical _____ to back it.
5. The _____ noise from the jackhammer lasted all day.
6. The company was _____ in sending out the order promptly.
7. The farmers were warned about a new species of aphids that _____ a strong strain of virus.
8. My grandparents asked that I send a _____ every week while I was away at college.

34 MONO—one

There are two roots meaning *one*—UNI (as in **unanimous**, **unify**, **unison**) and MONO. MONO is found is such words as **monoplane** (having only *one* pair of wings), **monarchy** (having *one* ruler), and **monotheism** (belief in *one* God). Two words we don't usually think of as containing MONO are monk and monastery. A **monk** was originally *one* religious man living alone, and a **monastery** was a dwelling place for monks living in seclusion from the world.

monarchy (mahn´ ahr key) [MONO one + ARCH ruler] noun—a government with one hereditary ruler. *At the end of the war, the monarchy became a democracy.*

monastery (mahn´ uh ster ē) noun—a dwelling place for monks living secluded from the world. *The monastery was high in the mountains.*

monk (munk) noun—originally, one religious man living alone; now, a member of a religious brotherhood living in a monastery. *The monks prayed in the sanctuary.*

monocle (mon´ uh kul) [MONO onbe + OCUL eye] noun—an eyeglass for one eye. *The English gentleman looked at us through his monocle.*

monogamy (muh nog´ uh mē) [MONO one + GAM marriage] noun—marriage to only one person at a time. *Monogamy is practiced in most countries today.*

monolith (mon´ uh lith) [MONO one + LITH stone] noun—one single large piece of stone, as a monument or a statue. *The monoliths at Stonehenge were transported from a great distance in prehistoric times.*

monopoly (muh nahp´ uh lē) [MONO one + POLY to sell] noun—exclusive control by one group of a commodity or service. *The student store had a monopoly on selling college sweatshirts.*

monosyllable (mon´ uh sil uh bul) noun—a word of one syllable. *She thought she had to speak to the child in monosyllables.*

monotheism (mon´ uh thē iz um) [MONO one + THE god] noun—the belief that there is only one God. *Unlike their neighbors, the early Hebrews held to monotheism.*

monotone (mon´ uh tōn) [MONO one + TON tone] noun—having one tone; lack of variety in tone. *Because the professor always spoke in a monotone, his students fell asleep.*

monotonous (mah nah´ tōn us) [MONO one + TON tone] adjective—literally one tone; having no variation. *Her constant complaints became monotonous.*

ALSO: monochromatic, monogamous, monogram, monograph, monolithic, monologue, mononucleosis, monoplane, monopolize, monorail, monotony

EXERCISE 1   Match the MONO word with its definition.

A. monotone   **B.** monosyllable   **C.** monogramy

D. monarchy   **E.** monotheism   **F.** monotonous

_____ **1.** the belief that there is only one God

_____ **2.** government with one hereditary ruler

_____ **3.** marriage to one person at a time

_____ **4.** a word of one syllable

_____ **5.** one tone

_____ **6.** having no variation

EXERCISE 2   Write the appropriate MONO word.

1. At least it's easy to tell where the accent falls in a _____.

2. _____ is the central belief of Christians, Jews, and Muslims.

3. Her speeches are boring because she speaks in a _____.

4. The island tribe practiced _____ and had strong taboos against marital infidelity.

5. The company was a _____, with a reputation for uniform policy in all its branches.

6. In Tonga, we saw the huge _____ (s) that had been set up in prehistoric times.

7. During the seventeenth century, most European countries were ruled by a _____.

8. Trying to look old-fashioned, he sported a pipe and _____.

9. During the Middle Ages, _____ (s) handwrote the Bible in Latin.

10. Wearing all one color of clothes is considered _____.

11. The _____ was built out of stone in the thirteenth century.

EXERCISE 3 JOURNAL   In your *vocabulary journal*, describe someone you know who is always complaining about ill health. Use some of these words: chronic, commiserate, malaise, dissuade, concur, malady.

35 | MORPH—form

MORPH meaning *form* is an easy root to spot and will help clarify some difficult words. For example, **amorphous** [A without + MORPH form] refers to something that is without *form*, such as a speech that has not yet been organized, a poem that is still in an unformed state, a plan that has not yet taken shape, or some clay that is ready for the potter's wheel.

amorphous (uh mawr′ fus) [A without + MORPH form] adjective—without definite form or shape. *His notes for his lecture were still in an amorphous state, without any plan or organization.*

anthropomorphism (an thruh po mawr′ fism) [ANTHROP human + MORPH form] noun—assigning human characteristics or behavior to inanimate objects or animals. *Most folktales, such as "The Ugly Duckling" and "The Fox and the Grapes," use anthropomorphism.*

ectomorph (ek tuh mawrf′) [ECTO outside + MORPH form] noun—person with a slender physical build developed from the inside layer of the embryo. *Tall, thin models are ectomorphs.*

endomorph (en duh mawrf′) [ENDO inside + MORPH form] noun—person with a prominent abdomen and other soft body parts developed from the inside layer of the embryo. *As an endomorph, I appreciated her curvy body.*

mesomorph (mez uh mawr′) [MESO middle + MORPH form] noun—person with a muscular or athletic build developed from the middle layer of the embryo. *Michael Phelps is a mesomorph, athletic and muscular.*

metamorphosis (met uh mawr′ fuh sis) [META change + MORPH form] noun—change of form or shape. *A caterpillar undergoes a metamorphosis when it turns into a butterfly.*

Morpheus (mawr′ fē us) noun—in Greek mythology, the god of dreams and of the forms that dreaming sleepers see. *Morpheus was so named because of the forms he controlled in people's dreams.*

morphine (mawr′ fēn) noun—a drug used to bring sleep or ease pain (named after Morpheus). *The doctor prescribed morphine for my agonizing pain.*

morphology (mawr fol′ uh je) [MORPH form + -LOGY study of] noun—the branch of biology that studies the form and structure of organisms; in language, the study of the structure and form of words. *The zoology professor specializes in the morphology of gophers.*

ALSO: anthropomorphic, anthropomorphism, metamorphic

✎ **EXERCISE 1**   Write the appropriate MORPH word.

1. Marilyn Monroe and Elizabeth Taylor were both _____, curvy and soft.

2. We can clarify words by their _____.

3. _____ is used to help ease severe chronic pain in cancer patients.

4. Athletes tend to be _____, strong athletic bodies.

5. Teachers with _____ lessons are hard to follow in a lecture.

6. _____ are slender and envied by many dieters.

7. We observed the _____ of the tadpole into a frog.

8. _____, the Greek god of dreams, still visits us nightly.

✎ **EXERCISE 2**   Write a sentence of your own for each MORPH word.

1. amorphous _____

_____

_____

2. metamorphosis _____

_____

_____

3. morphine _____

_____

_____

4. morphology _____

_____

_____

5. anthropomorphism _____

_____

_____

✎ **EXERCISE 3 WORD LIST**   Add a few more words to your **WORD LIST**, and then read over your list. Try to use a few of the words in your daily conversation.

EXTRA PRACTICE A, AN—MORPH

EXERCISE 1 Give the root that is used in each underlined word.

1. _____ To <u>exonerate</u> is to pardon.

2. _____ I feel no <u>malice</u> toward my former husband.

3. _____ <u>Ornithology</u> is the study of birds.

4. _____ They have <u>diverse</u> interests; he likes music and she likes sports.

5. _____ To <u>eradicate</u> is literally to tear out by the roots.

6. _____ <u>Equilateral</u> means each side is equal in a triangle.

7. _____ The refugee's <u>progeny</u> came from Siberia and settled in the Northwest.

8. _____ A <u>loquacious</u> person talks too much.

9. _____ A <u>prologue</u> comes at the beginning of a play.

10. _____ _____ The <u>philanthropist</u> was so <u>benevolent</u> that he gave his money to help people suffering from Hurricane Sandy.

11. _____ An <u>ambiguous</u> answer is very vague and therefore unclear.

12. _____ The <u>parameters</u> one should follow are in the instructions.

13. _____ Creative writers use <u>hyperbole</u> for humorous effect.

14. _____ The study of <u>monotheism</u> is important to religious leaders.

15. _____ The <u>premise</u> of her argument was sound.

EXERCISE 2 Give the meaning of each root and a word in which it is found.

ROOT	MEANING	WORD
1. A, AN	_____	_____
2. AMBI, AMPHI	_____	_____
3. ANN, ENN	_____	_____
4. ANTE, ANTI	_____	_____
5. ANTHROP	_____	_____
6. ANTI	_____	_____
7. AUTO	_____	_____
8. BENE	_____	_____
9. BI	_____	_____
10. BIO	_____	_____
11. CEDE, CEED	_____	_____
12. CHRON	_____	_____
13. CIRCUM	_____	_____

14. COGNI, GNOS   _____   _____

15. COM, CON, COL, COR   _____   _____

16. CRED   _____   _____

17. CUR   _____   _____

18. DEM   _____   _____

19. DICT   _____   _____

20. DIS, DI, DIF   _____   _____

21. EQU   _____   _____

22. EU   _____   _____

23. EX, ES, E   _____   _____

24. FID   _____   _____

25. GEN   _____   _____

26. GRAPH, GRAM   _____   _____

27. HYPER   _____   _____

28. LOG   _____   _____

29. LOGY   _____   _____

30. LOQU, LOC   _____   _____

31. MAL   _____   _____

32. METER, METR   _____   _____

33. MIT, MIS, MISS   _____   _____

34. MONO   _____   _____

35. MORPH   _____   _____

QUIZ YOURSELF **Visit the student companion website at www.cengagebrain.com to check your progress by working with the audio flashcards.**

In his epic poem *Paradise Lost,* John Milton calls the capital of hell **Pandemonium** (PAN all + DAIMON demon), the home of *all* demons, a place of wild confusion and noise. Today **pandemonium** has come to mean any wild uproar or tumult.

panacea (pan uh se´ uh) [PAN all + AKOS remedy] noun—a remedy or cure all for all ills or difficulties. *People who join cults are often looking for a panacea for their troubles.*

Pan-American (pan uh mer´ uh kun) noun—including all of America, both North and South. *He hopes to participate in the Pan-American Games.*

pandemic (pan dem´ ik) [PAN all + DEM people] adjective—literally among all the people; widespread. *The AIDS virus is pandemic.*

pandemonium (pan duh mo´ ne um) [PAN all + DAIMON demon] noun—literally the home of all demons in Milton's *Paradise Lost*; a wild uproar. *When the winning team returned, there was pandemonium.*

panoply (pan´ uh ple) [PAN all + HOPLON armor] noun—any magnificent or impressive array; a full suit of armor; ceremonial attire. *The woods in their full panoply of autumn foliage are an invitation to photographers.*

panorama (pan uh ram´ uh) [PAN all + HORAMA sight] noun—a view in all directions. *The panorama from the top of the Royal Gorge was awe-inspiring.*

pantheism (pan´ thē iz um) [PAN all + THE god] noun—the doctrine that God is all the laws and forces of nature and the universe. *He turned from the formal religions to a belief in pantheism.* Also, the ancient belief in and worship of all gods. *Pantheism was the religion of early Rome.*

pantheon (pan´ thē on) [PAN all + THE god] noun—a temple of all the gods. *They visited the Pantheon in Rome.* Also, the place of the idols of any group, or the idols themselves. *Aly Raisman's gold-medal performance entered her into the pantheon of American Olympic heroes.*

pantomime (pan´ tuh mīm) [PAN all + MIM to imitate] noun—a theatrical performance in which the actors play all the parts with gestures and without speaking. *Marcel Marceau turned the ancient dramatic form of pantomime into an art.*

ALSO: panchromatic, panegyric

✎ **EXERCISE 1** In your *vocabulary journal*, describe an excursion you have taken using some of the PAN words you just learned.

✎ **EXERCISE 2** Write the appropriate PAN word.

1. The 20 five-year-olds caused _____ at the birthday party.
2. The medicine was supposed to be a _____ for all diseases.
3. His love of nature and reverence for natural laws amounted to _____.
4. From the top of the cathedral we saw the _____ of the city.
5. _____ by a good actor can be as expressive as dialogue.
6. The marching band was out on the football field in their full _____.
7. His goal was to make the _____ of famous tennis players.
8. The delegates at the _____ Conference discussed trade, cooperation, and other issues of importance for the Americas.
9. There was a great fear that the H1N1 flu would become _____.

✎ **EXERCISE 3 REVIEW** The words in these sentences contain the roots you have studied. Put a C in front of each sentence in which all words are used correctly.

1. _____ The bald eagle, an amphibian, is the national bird of the United States.
2. _____ Metacognition is an awareness of one's own thinking and learning process.
3. _____ My mother plants perennials so she won't have to buy new plants each year.
4. _____ An endemic plant is one that is widespread over the entire earth.
5. _____ Our contestant found that he faced a powerful antagonist.
6. _____ Ayers Rock in Australia is the largest monolith in the world.
7. _____ The present queen is a benign monarch, always thinking of her subjects' welfare.
8. _____ Do you expect the self-help group to be a hypertrophy for all your problems?
9. _____ Her chronic cough has lasted for years.
10. _____ She is so to the point because she uses so many circumlocutions.

37 PATH—feeling, suffering

Do you feel sympathy or empathy when the schoolboy on stage has forgotten his speech? And do you feel apathy or antipathy toward the ideas a lecturer is presenting?

All four words—sympathy, empathy, apathy, and antipathy—describe *feelings* because they all contain the root PATH *feeling*. **Sympathy** [SYM together + PATH feeling) is literally *feeling* together with someone. **Empathy** [EM in + PATH feeling] is a stronger word, indicating that you identify with someone so closely that you *feel* "in" that person's position. **Apathy** [A without + PATH feeling] means lack of *feeling*, indifference. **Antipathy** [ANTI against + PATH feeling] means a *feeling* against someone or something, a strong dislike.

You will, of course, feel sympathy for the boy who is having stage fright, but if he happens to be your child, you will also feel empathy—identifying with him and participating in his suffering.

If the ideas a lecturer is presenting are boring, you'll feel apathy or indifference. You'll be apathetic, without feeling. But if you strongly disagree with the ideas, then you'll feel antipathy toward them and perhaps even toward the lecturer.

antipathy (an tip´ uh thē) [ANTI against + PATH feeling] noun—a feeling against someone or something; a strong dislike. *His antipathy toward those who disagreed with him was obvious.*

apathetic (ap uh thet´ ik) [A without + PATH feeling] adjective—without feeling; indifferent. *When Mandy failed to get a promotion, she became apathetic about her job and no longer did her best.*

apathy (ap´ uh thē) [A without + PATH feeling] noun—a lack of feeling; indifference. *Voter apathy was to blame for the poor turnout on Election Day.*

empathy (em´ puh thē) [EM in + PATH feeling] noun—an understanding so intimate that one participates in or identifies with another's feelings. *When Millie became widowed, Ruth showed her empathy to her dear friend.*

pathetic (puh thet´ ik) adjective—arousing feelings of pity. *The dog's hunt for her missing pups was pathetic.*

pathology (pa thol´ uh je) [PATH suffering + -LOGY study of] noun—the scientific study of the nature of a disease, especially the structural and functional changes caused by the disease, both physical and/or psychological. *Rather than treating patients, the doctor preferred doing laboratory research in pathology because he found studying the structure and function of damaged cells to be more challenging.*

pathos (pa´ thos) noun—a quality, in literature, film, music, dance, art, that arouses feelings of pity. *The audience was moved by the pathos of the character in the play as she overcame all the adversity she suffered.*

sympathy (sim´ puh thē) [SYM together + PATH feeling] noun—literally a feeling together with someone or something; a feeling for another person. *The coach felt sympathy for the girl who lost the race.*

telepathy (tuh lep´ uh thē) [TELE far + PATH feeling] noun—literally far feeling; the supposed communication between two people far apart by other than normal sensory means. *Because they so often thought of the same thing at the same time, they were convinced it was telepathy.*

ALSO: pathogenic, pathological, psychopath, psychopathic

✎ **EXERCISE 1   Write the PATH word next to its definition.**

1. _____ the supposed communication between two people far apart by other than normal sensory means
2. _____ without feeling; indifferent
3. _____ identifies in another's feelings
4. _____ arousing feelings of pity
5. _____ feeling for another person

✎ **EXERCISE 2   Write the appropriate PATH word. One word can be used twice.**

1. She feels such _____ for her son in his struggle to make the team that it is almost as if she were trying to make it herself.
2. The study of _____ helps advance new treatments in hepatitis research.
3. The girl wants to believe that her palm reader used _____ to "contact" her deceased father.
4. That haughty lawyer has a(n) _____ for his opponents.
5. The president expressed _____ for the Guatemalan people after the devastating earthquake.
6. Shakespeare's love poems arouse _____ in all of us.
7. Since Hector lost his job, he has become so _____ that he refuses to look for another job.
8. Mark's failure to attend college did not reflect his ability, but rather his _____ toward his education.
9. We decided my cousin was _____ when she stubbornly refused to change her bad habits.
10. Her habit of lying was diagnosed as a mental _____.

38 PED—foot

Two words containing PED were originally concerned with getting one's *foot* in an entanglement. **Impede** [IM in + PED foot] meant to get one's *foot* into an entanglement and thus hinder one's progress. Through the years, it has lost the meaning of the foot in an entanglement and now has come to mean merely to hinder the progress of. **Expedite** [EX out + PED foot] originally meant to get one's *foot* out of an entanglement and thus to speed up one's progress. Expedite too has lost that particular meaning and today means merely to speed the progress of, to help along. You might say that a poor vocabulary will impede your progress in college, whereas a large vocabulary will expedite your progress by helping you read with more understanding.

expedient (ek spē de unt) [EX out + PED foot] adjective—advantageous; useful in getting a desired result. *It is expedient to start writing your paper long before it is due.*

expedite (ek′ spuh dīt) [EX out + PED foot] verb—to speed the progress of; to help along. *To expedite your registration, fill out the forms ahead of time.*

expedition (ek spuh dish′ un) [EX out + PED foot] noun—a journey for a definite purpose. *The expedition to the North Pole brought back much scientific information.*

impede (im pēd′) [IM in + PED foot] verb—to cause delay, interrupt, or make difficult. *An inability to read with comprehension may impede one's academic progress.*

impediment (im ped′ uh munt) [IM in + PED foot] noun—anything that delays or interrupts. *The famous Greek orator Demosthenes had to overcome a speech impediment.*

pedestrian (pu des′ tre un) [PED foot] noun—one who goes on foot. *This is a dangerous corner for pedestrians.* Also as an adjective; commonplace or dull, as in a pedestrian style of writing. *Because of my numerous food allergies, I eat a pedestrian diet.*

pedigree (ped′ uh grē) [from the French PIED foot + DE of + GRUE crane] noun—a record of ancestry or genealogical chart because the chart's lines look like a crane's foot. *The collie's pedigree made him a valuable show dog.*

ALSO: biped, centipede, pedal, pedestal, pedicure, pedometer, quadruped

✎ **EXERCISE 1 JOURNAL** In your *vocabulary journal*, write two sentences that show how your progress has been impeded in mastering the words in this book and two sentences that show how your progress has been expedited in mastering the words in this book.

✎ **EXERCISE 2** Write the PED word next to its definition.

1. _____ a record of ancestry or genealogical chart

2. _____ one who goes on foot

3. _____ commonplace or dull

4. _____ a journey for a definite purpose

5. _____ to cause delay, interrupt, or make difficult

6. _____ advantageous

7. _____ anything that delays, interrupts

8. _____ to speed the progress of

✎ **EXERCISE 3   Write the appropriate PED word.**

1. Reading my reference materials ahead of time will _____ my progress in writing my paper.

2. The junior salesperson thought it might be _____ to invite the boss to dinner.

3. Spraining his ankle early in the season is going to _____ his chances of winning the championship.

4. Kim couldn't imagine anyone wanting a dog without a _____.

5. His unpopular voting record is a(n) _____ in his reelection campaign.

6. The mountaineers' _____ ended in triumph.

7. Often, teachers will comment that their students' writing is _____, rather than say "boring."

✎ **EXERCISE 4 REVIEW   Using the following five words, fill in the blanks in the paragraph so that it makes sense. After checking your answers, reread the paragraph and see how satisfying it is to read a paragraph in which you are sure of all the words.**

beneficiaries	census	apathy
expedite	demographic	

The results of the 2010 _____ have given us a _____ picture of the United States. Census forms were mailed to each dwelling to _____ the task of counting the entire population. Advertising was used to overcome the _____ that might have kept people from filling out the forms. The facts gathered were especially important to cities and states with population increases, for they are now the _____ of increased funding from government programs.

A word containing PHIL will have something to do with *love*. **Philosophy** [PHIL to love + SOPH wise] is the *love* of wisdom. A **bibliophile** [BIBL book + PHIL to love] is one who *loves* books. And a **philanthropist** [PHIL to love + ANTHROP human] is one who *loves* human beings, particularly one who gives money to benefit humanity (see page 20).

bibliophile (bib´ le uh f īl) [BIBL book + PHIL to love] noun—one who loves books; a book collector. *We discovered a bookstore with a panoply of books; it was obviously owned by a true bibliophile.*

philanthropist (fi lan´ thruh pist) [PHIL to love + ANTHROP human] noun—literally one who loves people; charitable person, particularly one who gives money to benefit humanity. *Philanthropist Doris Duke gave money to build beautiful public gardens.*

philharmonic (fil hahr mon´ ik) [PHIL to love + HARMONIA harmony] adjective—literally loving harmony; devoted to music; a symphony orchestra. *Last winter we heard the Chicago Philharmonic Orchestra.*

philodendron (fil uh den´ drun) [PHIL to love + DENDR tree] noun—a tropical climbing plant that likes the shade of other larger trees. *She cultivated the philodendron plant for its showy, heart-shaped leaves in her shade garden.*

philosopher (fi los´ uh fur) [PHIL to love + SOPH wise] noun—one who loves and pursues wisdom through logic and reasoning. *Immanuel Kant was one of the great philosophers of the eighteenth century.*

philosophy (fi los´ uh fē) [PHIL to love + SOPH wise] noun—the love and pursuit of wisdom through reasoning. *Socrates, considered the "father" of philosophy, formed our ways of using logical reasoning to understand "truth."*

ALSO: Anglophile, Philadelphia, philanthropy, philatelist, philippic, philology

EXERCISE 1   Match each PHIL word with its definition.

A. philharmonic	**C.** philodendron	**E.** philosophy
B. bibliophile	**D.** philosopher	**F.** philanthropist

1. _____ one who loves books

2. _____ tropical climbing plant

3. _____ one who loves human beings and gives money to benefit humanity

4. _____ one who loves and pursues wisdom through reasoning

5. _____ loving harmony, devoted to music, a symphony orchestra

6. _____ the love and pursuit of wisdom through reasoning

✏️ **EXERCISE 2   Write the appropriate PHIL word.**

1. The _____ loves everything about books, including their bindings and illustrations.
2. Socrates wrote, "This sense of wonder is the mark of the _____."
3. "The building's acoustics are perfect for a _____ hall," said the musician.
4. Educator Maria Montessori's _____ was that we should encourage children's natural desire to learn.
5. The _____ is one of the world's most popular tropical plants.
6. _____ (s) make our world better by their generosity.

✏️ **EXERCISE 3 REVIEW   Underline the appropriate word.**

1. The study of the forms of animals and plants is called (morphology, pathology).
2. Through her study of (entomology, etymology), she has learned the derivation of many words and thus improved her vocabulary.
3. The company was a (monopoly, monologue), with a strong central office controlling their branches.
4. He took a course in (choreography, calligraphy) to improve his penmanship.
5. The cashier was accused of (malnutrition, malfeasance) when the deficit was discovered.
6. She felt (apathy, antipathy) toward the course, hating every moment of it.
7. The actor used (pantomime, panacea) rather than words to present the character.
8. An interest in word roots will (impede, expedite) your learning new words.
9. The supervisor found the employee guilty of one lie after another and branded him (credulous, perfidious).
10. Saying that entering a new college is like jumping into an icy lake is an (analogy, anecdote).
11. The (graffiti, hologram) on the card was a beautiful example of 3-D art.
12. Samuel Alderson, the inventor of the crash dummy, was added to the (panoply, pantheon) of famous inventors.
13. The census has brought about a more (equivocal, equitable) distribution of government funds.
14. He was (remiss, premise) in not returning the library book in a timely manner.
15. Being (hyperopic, hyperbaton), she always keeps her glasses nearby.

40 PHOB—fear

Do you refuse to stand on the observation platform of a tall building? If so, perhaps you have **acrophobia**, an excessive *fear* of high places. Do you avoid elevators? If so, you may be suffering from **claustrophobia**, an excessive *fear* of closed places.

acrophobia (ak ruh fo´ be uh) [ACRO high + PHOB fear] noun—an excessive or illogical fear of high places. *Because of her acrophobia, she refused to approach the rim of the canyon.*

agoraphobia (ag ruh fo' be uh) [AGOR marketplace + PHOB fear] noun—an anxiety disorder when the person suffers from and is fearful of open or public spaces. *Janice had severe agoraphobia and would not drive over the Golden Gate Bridge while visiting San Francisco.*

claustrophobia (klos truh fo´ be uh) [CLAUS to close + PHOB fear] noun—an excessive or illogical fear of enclosed places. *His claustrophobia made him prefer an office that opened onto a balcony.*

hydrophobia (hi druh fo´ be uh) [HYDR water + PHOB fear] noun—an abnormal fear of water. Also, rabies (rabies was first called hydrophobia because victims were unable to swallow water). *There was an outbreak of hydrophobia among the dogs of the area.*

phobia (fo´ be uh) noun—an excessive or illogical fear of some particular thing or situation. *Her fear of germs has really become a phobia.*

phobic (fo´ bik) adjective—excessively fearful. *She had a phobic need to avoid large crowds.*

photophobia (fo tuh fo´ be uh) [PHOT light + PHOB fear] noun—an abnormal intolerance of light; light sensitive. *Because of photophobia, he had to wear tinted glasses.*

technophobia (tek nuh fo´ be uh) [TECHN skill + PHOB fear] noun—a fear of technology; computer anxiety. *She finally overcame her technophobia and completed a course called "Introduction to Computers."*

xenophobia (zen uh fo´ be uh) [XENO foreigner + PHOB fear] noun—fear or hatred of foreigners or strangers; prejudice of others. *Extreme patriotism may turn into xenophobia.*

EXERCISE 1   Match the PHOB word with its definition.

1. _____ phobic

2. _____ xenophobia

3. _____ hydrophobia

4. _____ acrophobia

5. _____ claustrophobia

6. _____ agoraphobia

7. _____ technophobia

8. _____ phobia

A. fear of open or public spaces

B. an excessive or illogical fear of high places

C. excessively fearful

D. an excessive or illogical fear of enclosed places

E. fear or hatred of foreigners or strangers

F. an abnormal fear of water

G. an excessive or illogical fear of a particular thing or situation

H. a fear of technology

✎ **EXERCISE 2   Write the appropriate PHOB word.**

1. His eye problems were diagnosed as _____.

2. Because of his _____, he had a dread of falling that made him constantly uneasy.

3. Their lack of understanding of foreigners amounted to _____.

4. She claimed she got _____ working in a small room with no windows.

5. Raccoons can sometimes be the carriers of _____.

6. Many elderly people are anxious about computers and the Internet; they have _____.

7. Her fear of many different things amounts to a general _____.

8. Without the right help, dyslexic children can become _____ of school.

9. Because of his _____ he is completely housebound.

✎ **EXERCISE 3 REVIEW   Write the correct word for each sentence from the following list.**

analogy	hyperactive	bicameral	morphology
loquacious	disproportionate	expedite	

1. The child's _____ behavior made it difficult for her to sit still in class.

2. The students study the _____ of cells in their biology class.

3. Samuel Johnson's quote, "Dictionaries are like watches; the worst is better than none, and the best cannot be expected to go quite true" is an _____.

4. The United States House of Representatives and the Senate are _____ legal systems of our three branches of government.

5. It took Della an hour to get off the phone with the _____ salesman; he talked the whole time.

6. The claims adjuster promised to _____ our claim after Hurricane Sandy.

7. My brother took a _____ piece of birthday cake, leaving a little for the rest of the guests.

✎ **EXERCISE 4 WORD LIST   Are you adding words to your WORD LIST? Regularly adding words will increase your vocabulary. Use a word three times and it is yours.**

EXTRA PRACTICE A, AN—PHOB

EXERCISE 1 Match each word with its definition.

A. biennial   **C.** anthropoid   **E.** amorphous   **G.** topography   **I.** disconsolate

B. chronic   **D.** benevolent   **F.** anthropologist   **H.** perimeter   **J.** malaise

1. _____ inclined to do good
2. _____ without definite form or shape
3. _____ occurring every two years
4. _____ resembling human beings
5. _____ one who studies the development and behavior of human beings
6. _____ continuing for a long time
7. _____ detailed drawing or map of a surface or region
8. _____ unable to be consoled; hopelessly sad
9. _____ vague feeling of illness or depression
10. _____ boundary around an area

EXERCISE 2 Write C in front of each sentence in which all words are used correctly.

1. _____ Lewis and Clark's expedition took them across the continental United States.
2. _____ The metronome helped the piano student keep to the beat of the music.
3. _____ We found that the problem was an impediment and so could easily be solved with little effort.
4. _____ After I lost that tennis match, I was in a state of euphoria.
5. _____ He has always been confident and dreads speaking in public.
6. _____ Unfortunately, we omitted the prospectus to the potential clients.
7. _____ We are looking for a pedestrian house, one with at least ten rooms and a triple garage.
8. _____ The director tried to influence the board members, but they were circumspect of his efforts.
9. _____ He enervated his success to hard work and a bit of luck.
10. _____ The bride cast a malevolent glance at the guest who arrived in combat boots and a trench coat.

EXERCISE 3 Give the meaning of each root and a word in which it is found.

ROOT	MEANING	WORD
1. A, AN	_____	_____
2. ANTHROP	_____	_____
3. ANTE, ANTI	_____	_____
4. AUTO	_____	_____

5. BENE _____ _____

6. CEDE _____ _____

7. COGNI, GNOS _____ _____

8. COM, CON, COL, COR _____ _____

9. CUR _____ _____

10. DICT _____ _____

11. DIS, DI, DIF _____ _____

12. EQU _____ _____

13. EU _____ _____

14. EX, ES, E _____ _____

15. FID _____ _____

16. GEN _____ _____

17. GRAPH, GRAM _____ _____

18. HYPER _____ _____

19. LOG _____ _____

20. -LOGY _____ _____

21. LOQU, LOC _____ _____

22. MAL _____ _____

23. METER, METR _____ _____

24. MIT, MIS, MISS _____ _____

25. MONO _____ _____

26. MORPH _____ _____

27. PAN _____ _____

28. PATH _____ _____

29. PED _____ _____

30. PHIL _____ _____

31. PHOB _____ _____

QUIZ YOURSELF   Visit the student companion website at www.cengagebrain.com
to check your progress by working with the audio flashcards.

41 PHON—sound

Any word containing PHON always has something to do with *sound*. A **symphony** [SYM together + PHON sound] is literally *sounds* together, presumably pleasant sounds. If a *sound* is harsh or unpleasant, it is called **cacophony** [CACO bad + PHON sound], whereas smooth and harmonious *sounds,* especially words or phrases that please the ear, are called **euphony** [EU good + PHON sound].

cacophony (ka kof′ uh nē) [CACO bad + PHON sound] noun—disagreeable or discordant sounds. *Only a mother can enjoy the cacophony of her child's violin practice.*

euphonious (yO fo′ nē us) [EU good + PHON sound] adjective—having a pleasant sound; harmonious. *The euphonious sounds of the chorus ended the musical performance on a high note.*

phonetics (fuh net′ iks) noun—the branch of language study dealing with speech sounds and their symbols. *Knowledge of phonetics is an aid in learning to speak a new language.*

phonics (fon′ iks) noun—the use of the sounds of letters and groups of letters in teaching beginners to read. *The teacher used phonics to teach the children to sound out words.*

polyphonic (pol ē fon′ ik) [POLY many + PHON sound] adjective—having or making many sounds; representing more than one sound, such as c in cat and cereal. *The first polyphonic synthesizers, available in the 1970s, created a complex sound.*

saxophone (sak′ suh fōn) [SAX (after Adolphe Sax, the inventor) + PHON sound] noun— a wind instrument. *My brother learned to control his breath while playing the saxophone.*

symphony (sim′ fuh nē) [SYM together + PHON sound] noun—literally sounds together; a harmony of sounds; an orchestra; music written for an orchestra. *Beethoven was the first major composer to use voices in a symphony.*

ALSO: antiphonal, euphony, megaphone, microphone, phonograph, stereophonic, telephone

EXERCISE 1   Match the word with its definition.

1. _____ cacophony

2. _____ phonetics

3. _____ symphony

4. _____ phonics

5. _____ euphonious

6. _____ polyphonic

7. _____ saxophone

A. having pleasant sounds

B. an orchestra playing together

C. the use of the sounds of letters and groups of letters in teaching beginners to read

D. bad sounds, disagreeable

E. the branch of language study dealing with speech sounds and their symbols

F. a wind instrument

G. having or making many sounds

✎ **EXERCISE 2   Write the appropriate PHON word.**

1. It was good to get out of the _____ of the office with its ringing phone and chattering people.

2. The several melodies are combined into a _____ symphony.

3. The _____ was named after its inventor, Adolphe Sax.

4. Beethoven's Ninth _____ is one of the most beautiful musical compositions of all time.

5. His knowledge of _____ helped him pronounce French words correctly.

6. In the movie *Cinderella*, Cinderella's _____ voice matches her sweet personality

7. Many children learn to read successfully through the _____ method.

✎ **EXERCISE 3 REVIEW   Underline the appropriate word.**

1. The prisoner was (exonerated, eradicated) from the courts after the DNA evidence proved his innocence.

2. Only a (ventriloquist, bibliophile) would be interested in that tattered old book.

3. Cheating and lying are forms of (perfidy, fidelity).

4. The two countries agreed on the (bilateral, bilingual) pact.

5. Her college course in (ornithology, anthropology) led to her lifelong hobby of bird watching.

6. The (premise, soliloquy) of the argument was supported by valid evidence.

7. I won't let anything (expedite, impede) my progress in learning new words.

8. We (exonerated, expurgated) the offensive language from the manuscript.

9. No one with (acrophobia, claustrophobia) will want to go into the cave.

10. The secretary felt (circumvented, circumscribed) by all the regulations she had to follow.

11. A (malcontent, philanthropist) brought food aid to the displaced people in Syria.

✎ **EXERCISE 4 JOURNAL   In your *vocabulary journal*, write sentences that show the best examples of cacophony, euphony, and symphony that you can think of.**

Preposterous is made up of PRE *before* and POST *after* and originally meant having the before part where the after part should be, as a horse with its head where its tail should be. Such a *before-after* animal would be preposterous or absurd. And so today, anything contrary to nature, reason, or common sense is called preposterous.

postdate (pōs dāt´) [POST after + DATE date] verb—to date a check or other document with a future date rather than the actual date. *Because I had no money in the bank, I postdated my check.*

posterior (pō stir´ e ur) adjective—located behind (as opposed to anterior, located in front). *The posterior legs of the jackrabbit are stronger than the anterior ones.*

posterity (po ster´ uh tē) noun—those who come after; future generations. *Posterity will determine the value of his writing.*

postgraduate (post graj´ uh wut) adjective—relating to a course of study after college graduation. *I look forward to taking a couple of postgraduate courses after I complete my undergraduate degree.*

posthumously (pos´ choo mus li) adverb—after the death of the father, as a child born posthumously; after the death of the author, as a book published posthumously; after one's death, as an award received posthumously. *The Medal of Honor was awarded to the war chaplain posthumously.*

Post-impressionist (post im presh´ uh nist) noun—after the Impressionists; a school of painting in France in the late nineteenth century that followed the Impressionists. *Cézanne and Matisse were Post-impressionist painters.*

postlude (post´ lOd) [POST after + LUD to play] noun—a piece of music played after a church service. *The organist played a Bach fugue as a postlude.*

post meridiem (post muh ridé ē um) [POST after + MERIDI noon] noun—(abbreviated P.M.) after noon. *The committee will meet at 3 P.M.*

postmortem (post mor´ tum) [POST after + MORT death] noun—an examination after death; an autopsy. *The postmortem revealed the cause of his death.*

postscript (pō skript) [POST after + SCRIPT to write] noun—a note written after the main body of a letter (abbreviated P.S.). *Often the most interesting part of her letter was the postscript.*

preposterous (pri pos´ tur us) [PRE before + POST after] adjective—contrary to nature, reason, or common sense; absurd. *The idea of flying to the moon was once considered preposterous.*

ALSO: postnatal, postnuptial, postoperative, postpone

✎ EXERCISE 1   Write the appropriate POST word.

1. Now that the poet has died, some of his poems are being published _____.
2. They prepared a time capsule for _____.
3. Traveling faster than sound was once considered _____.
4. The _____ of female baboons are red to attract males.
5. During the organ _____, the congregation left the church.
6. An entire gallery in the New York Metropolitan Art Museum is devoted to the works of the _____, Seurat, *Cézanne,* and Van Gogh.
7. Because the death was unexpected, a _____ was required.
8. Banks often do not notice whether or not a check has been _____(ed).
9. After receiving her Bachelor of Arts degree, she enrolled in a _____ degree program in electrical engineering.
10. Ante meridiem is usually when I wake, and _____ is when I go to sleep.
11. The hastily written _____ showed it was an afterthought.

✎ EXERCISE 2 REVIEW   Underline the appropriate word.

1. Only filled with (benevolence, malevolence), the teacher spent hours helping the immigrants.
2. He would (eulogize, excoriate) his wife for the slightest error in her cooking.
3. They talked about subjects as (disparate, equivalent) as mud pies and ballet.
4. The applicant tended to (equivocate, expurgate) when his former job was mentioned.
5. I was (credulous, disconcerted) when they excluded me from their plans.
6. A distrust of foreigners is called (technophobia, xenophobia).
7. The government was constantly threatened by the (dissident, diffident).
8. The (bipartisan, bilingual) teacher translated the poem from Spanish to English.
9. The manager of the hotel tried to create an (ambivalence, ambience) of luxury.
10. The society planned (biannual, biennial) meetings so the members could see each other twice a year.
11. The organist played a (prologue, postlude) at the end of the service.
12. Cambodian Leader Pol Pot was a (demagogue, monastery) who murdered millions of his own people in the 1970s.
13. The surgeon examined the cells in the (pathology, phonetics) laboratory.
14. The (hyperactive, hypercritical) boy could not stop moving even after his teacher removed him from the group.
15. (Proceed, Recede) to the front of the line.

43 PRE—before

PRE at the beginning of a word always means *before* and is easy to understand in such words as **preschool**, **premature**, **prehistoric**, **premeditate**, **prejudge**, and **precaution**. But sometimes, the meaning is not so obvious. For example, **precocious** [PRE before + COQUERE to cook, to ripen] originally applied to fruit that ripened early (*before* time). Today, it describes someone who has matured earlier than usual, particularly mentally. Children who are unusually smart for their age are called **precocious**. They have ripened early!

preamble (pre´ am bul) [PRE before + AMBUL to walk] noun—a preliminary statement to a document. *Have you read the Preamble to the Constitution?*

precedent (pres´ uh dunt) [PRE before + CED to go] noun—an act that goes before and may serve as an example for later acts. *By giving his prize to charity, he set a precedent that later winners followed.*

precipitate (pri sip´ uh tāt) [PRE before + CAPIT head] verb—to bring about suddenly, rapidly; to hasten the occurrence of. *On March 19, 2013, the Cyprus government precipitated great panic once their banking system defaulted.*

precise (pri sis´) [PRE before + CIS to cut] adjective—sharply defined and exact. *Her descriptions were always precise.*

preclude (pri klOd´) [PRE before + CLUD to shut] verb—literally to shut out beforehand; to make impossible by a previous action; to prevent. *His poor record with that company may preclude his getting another job.*

precocious (pri ko´ shus) [PRE before + COQUERE to cook, ripen] adjective—prematurely developed, advanced in mental development, especially in children. *The child was precocious, having learned to read at two.*

preeminent (pre em´ uh nunt) [PRE before + EMINERE to stand out] adjective—standing out before all others. *Steve Jobs was preeminent among the computer inventors of his day.*

prejudice (prej´ ud us) [PRE before + JUD judge] noun—a judgment formed beforehand without examination of the facts. *She finally realized that her intolerance of the newcomers was simply unfounded prejudice.*

prelude (prel´ Od) [PRE before + LUD to play] noun—an introductory piece of music; a concert piece for piano or orchestra. *She played a Chopin prelude at the recital.* Also, an introductory performance or action preceding a more important one. *The passage of that law was the prelude to further civil rights legislation.*

preponderant (pri pon´ dur unt) [PRE before + PONDER weight] adjective—outweighing; having more power or importance. *The preponderant theme of the speakers was the future welfare of the institution.*

prerequisite (pre rek´ wuh zit) noun—something required beforehand. *Algebra is a prerequisite for geometry.*

presage (pres´ ij) [PRE before + SAGIRE to perceive] verb—to perceive beforehand; to predict. *Lack of cooperation among the employees presages trouble in the industry. Those dark clouds presage a storm.*

prevail (pri vāl´) [PRE before + VAL to be strong] verb—to be strong before all others; to win, as to prevail over the other contestants. *After years of practice, he finally prevailed over his challengers.*

ALSO: precede, precursor, predestination, predict, predilection, predominant, preempt, premise, preposterous, prerogative, prescribe, presentiment, preside, president, pretentious, prevent, previous, unprecedented

✎ **EXERCISE 1   Match the word with its definition.**

1. _____ precocious
2. _____ precise
3. _____ preclude
4. _____ preponderant
5. _____ presage

A. to prevent
B. to predict
C. sharply defined, exact
D. prematurely developed
E. outweighing; having more power or importance

✎ **EXERCISE 2   Write the appropriate PRE word.**

1. Meteorologists often use barometric pressure to _____ tornados.
2. She insisted that her child was _____ because of her early drawing ability.
3. The court decision set a _____ that was followed for many years.
4. After publishing her research, she was considered _____ in her field.
5. Most professional writers strive to use _____ language.
6. The _____ to the U.S. Constitution also explains its mission.
7. Most of us are _____ in some ways against those we do not know.
8. The U.S. military _____ (ed) in World War II.
9. The ability to drive a tractor is a _____ for the job.
10. The _____ to the symphony was euphonious.
11. The _____ message by the oil companies is that they are not to blame for the rising oil prices.
12. Working with your hands does not _____ using your head.

44   PRO—forward, before, for, forth

Do you tend to put off unpleasant tasks until a future time? If so, you probably have a **propensity** [PRO forward + PENS to hang] (a hanging *forward* or inclination) to **procrastinate** [PRO forward + CRAS tomorrow] noun—to push tasks *forward* until tomorrow. When it comes to studying, many students have a propensity to procrastinate.

proclaim (pro klām') [PRO forth + CLAM to cry out] verb—to announce officially or declare publicly. *The day was proclaimed a holiday.*

proclivity (pro kliv' uh tē) [PRO forward + CLIVUS slope] noun—an inclination toward something, natural or habitual tendency; propensity. *Her proclivity to exaggerate finally led to her losing her job.*

procrastinate (pro kras' tuh nāt) [PRO forward + CRAS tomorrow] verb—to put off doing something until a future time. *I always procrastinate about cleaning the house.*

profuse (pruh fyOs') [PRO forth + FUS to pour] adjective—pouring forth freely; generous. *The grandmother's profuse kisses embarrassed the child.*

promontory (prom' un tor ē) [PRO forward + MONT mountain] noun—a high peak of land or rock (mountain) jutting forward into the sea. *From the promontory, we had a view of the entire area.*

propensity (pruh pen' suh tē) [PRO forward + PENS to hang] noun—a natural inclination; proclivity. *He has a propensity for being highly organized.* (Propensity and proclivity are close synonyms.)

proponent (pruh po' nunt) [PRO before + PON to put] noun—one who argues in favor of something; an advocate. *A leading proponent of recycling is speaking tonight.*

prospectus (pruh spek' tus) [PRO forward + SPECT to look] noun—a printed description of a proposed document, plan, or contract. *The prospectus made the new subdivision look inviting.*

protuberant (pro tO' bur unt) [PRO forth + TUBER swelling] adjective—bulging. *From childhood he had been conscious of his protuberant nose.*

provident (prov' uh dunt) [PRO before + VID to see] noun—making provision for the future. *If he had been more provident, he wouldn't be in need now.*

ALSO: improvise, proceed, proclamation, produce, profusion, progenitor, progeny, prognosis, prognosticate, program, projectile, prologue, promotion, promulgate, pronoun, propel, prophet, propitiate, propitious, proposal, proscribe, protracted, provide, provision, provocation

EXERCISE 1   Write the appropriate PRO word.

1. The _____ for the investment fund was tempting.

2. His _____ or _____ for working efficiently may give him a bonus.

3. She's a _____ of the new national health plan that President Obama crafted with the Senate and House of Representatives.

4. Most endomorphs have _____ stomachs.

5. Whenever I _____, someone always quotes the old epigram, "Don't put off until tomorrow, what you can do today."

6. With _____ thanks, she accepted the award.

7. We stood on the _____ and looked out over Yosemite Valley.

8. Always a _____ person, she had taken care of her family's needs before she left for the month.

9. The accused man _____ (ed) his innocence.

EXERCISE 2 REVIEW   Match each word root with its meaning.

1. _____ PATH   **A.** after

2. _____ PED   **B.** foot

3. _____ PHIL   **C.** feeling, suffering

4. _____ PHOB   **D.** forward, before, for, forth

5. _____ PHON   **E.** before

6. _____ POST   **F.** to love

7. _____ PRE   **G.** sound

8. _____ PRO   **H.** fear

EXERCISE 3 JOURNAL   In your *vocabulary journal*, write a humorous paragraph using as many PRE and PRO words as possible.

What would you do with a recalcitrant child? First you might have to figure out the meaning of **recalcitrant**. Because RE means *back* and CALC means *heel,* recalcitrant means literally kicking *back* the heels. Once used in referring to horses and mules, it now is applied to human beings. Therefore, a recalcitrant child would be one who is kicking *back,* obstinate, stubbornly rebellious.

The meaning of many words that begin with RE are simple: **return** is simply to turn *again,* **recall** is to call *again,* and **reconstruct** is to construct *again.*

Here are some more familiar words for which you won't need pronunciation help or example sentences.

recede [RE back + CED to go] verb—to go back, as a river recedes from its banks.

receive [RE again + CAP to take] verb—to take something offered.

recreation [RE again + CREAT to create] noun—the refreshment of mind or body through some form of play or amusement.

referee [RE back + FER to carry] noun—one to whom questions are carried back; an official in a sports contest.

remit [RE back + MIT to send] verb—to send back, as to remit payment.

reside [RE back + SID to sit] verb—to dwell, as to reside in a house.

residue [RE back + SID to sit] noun—the part that remains after part has been separated away, as the residue in the bottom of a vase.

retain [RE back + TEN to hold] verb—to hold back or keep in one's possession.

revenue [RE back + VEN to come] noun—money that comes back from an investment or other source; taxes and other income collected by a government.

revise [RE again + VIS to see] verb—to see again in order to correct errors.

revive [RE again + VIV to live] verb—to cause to live again.

And here are some less familiar words.

recalcitrant (ri kal´ suh trunt) [RE back + CALC heel] adjective—obstinate; stubbornly rebellious. *It's useless to argue with her when she's in a recalcitrant mood.*

recant (ri kant´) [RE back + CANT to sing] verb—to renounce a belief formerly held, especially in a formal or public manner. *The judge chose to recant publicly his former stand on capital punishment.*

recession (ri sesh´ un) [RE back + CESS to go] noun—a period of reduced economic activity. *The government feared a business recession.*

recluse (rek´ lOs) [RE back + CLUS to shut] noun—one who lives shut back from the world. *The poet Emily Dickinson lived as a recluse in her house in Amherst.*

remiss (ri mis´) [RE back + MISS to send] adjective—negligent; lax in attending to duty. *I've been remiss about doing my exercises.*

Renaissance (ren´ uh sahns) [RE again + NASC to be born] noun—a rebirth; the revival of classical art, literature, and learning in Europe in the fourteenth, fifteenth, and sixteenth centuries. *Michelangelo was an artist of the Renaissance.* Also used to imply a rebirth. *Despite the damage caused by Hurricane Sandy, the Jersey Shore is experiencing a renaissance.*

resilience (ri zil´ yunts) [RE again + SIL to leap] noun—the ability to recover quickly from illness, change, or misfortune. *With her customary resilience, she bounced back after her long illness.*

revert (ri vurt´) [RE back + VERT to turn] verb—to return to a former habit or condition. *Occasionally, she would revert to her childhood dialect.*

ALSO: irrevocable, rebel, recapitulate, reclaim, recourse, recur, recurrent, reflect, refractory, reject, remission, repel, respect, retort, revoke, revolve

EXERCISE 1   Write the appropriate RE word.

1. They were afraid to make any investments for fear the _____ would continue.

2. He had never been an unruly or _____ child.

3. Occasionally, however, he would _____ to infant behavior.

4. One needs plenty of _____ to cope with all the disappointments in that job.

5. Because of the BP oil rig explosion, the oil spilled will not _____, but will flow into the Gulf of Mexico.

6. Living like a _____, he avoids all social contacts.

7. The best French and Italian painters emerged during the _____ period.

8. The candidate has taken such a strong stand that for him to _____ would be unthinkable.

9. The accountant was _____ at filing his own tax return and had to pay a late fee to the IRS.

10. He argued with the _____ over the call on the play.

11. My writing teacher reminded me that to _____ means to "see again."

12. The _____ center opened on Memorial Day.

13. We had to _____ the payment in full before they would let us take the furniture.

14. The school decided to _____ the Latin courses after an absence of ten years.

15. She will _____ the receipt in case she wants to return the item.

16. None of the samples tested were found to contain _____.

17. We all like to _____ presents on our birthday.

18. The _____ collected through taxes paid for the upgrades to the school.

EXERCISE 1 Underline each incorrect word in the following sentences. Then, in each blank, write the word that should have been used.

1. _____ Deciding to immigrate from their homeland, they moved to Canada.

2. _____ Federal laws are attempting to enervate sexual discrimination.

3. _____ They watched the smokestack expatiate pollutants.

4. _____ She embroidered her cardiogram on all her towels.

5. _____ The public was becoming aware of the premise in the mayor's speeches.

6. _____ You can count on his recalcitrance to help him make a comeback even when he loses.

7. _____ We were amazed at the provident of flowers in their garden.

8. _____ Queen Elizabeth is the present intercede in a long line of rulers.

9. _____ Scientists study the malfeasance of a tadpole into a frog.

10. _____ Some speakers are quite unconcerned with their monocle and sometimes speak unclearly.

EXERCISE 2 Using nine of the following twelve words, fill in the blanks in the paragraph so that it makes sense. Reread the paragraph and see how satisfying it is to read a paragraph in which you are sure of all the words.

diction	confident	preposterous	recede
presages	credible	apathetic	etymology
predict	ebullient	recourse	precise

I've read that a large vocabulary _____ success both in college and in one's career. The idea sounds _____, and I'm now taking more interest in _____. I see improvement in my vocabulary and _____. I am _____ about using new words. Sometimes my _____ friends think my new hobby is _____, but gradually even they are discovering the _____ feeling that comes from using _____ words.

EXERCISE 3 Here, taken from magazine articles, are sentences containing words you have studied. Underline the appropriate review word in each sentence and provide its meaning. Check in the Word Index for any words you don't remember.

1. St. Augustine, Florida, boasts it is the oldest city in the United States; many of its homes antedate the Revolutionary War. _____

2. The British prime minister excoriated the new Labour Party leaders. _____

3. Concerning his first experience with weightlessness, the astronaut said, "I was in an almost euphoric condition." _____

4. The president of the United Nations Security Council engendered the respect of the African delegation. _____

5. Gregory Hines highlighted the dance's meaning with a panoply of foot moves. _____

6. The deadly plague reached across the Mediterranean from Africa during the first pandemic, beginning in AD 541. _____

7. The senator predicts that gas prices will remain high. _____

8. The student's propensity to analyze literature is admirable. _____

9. She is cognizant of her responsibility to her parents. _____

10. The FCC's report contained a cacophony of conflicting claims, bewildering investors. _____

11. Two hundred researchers from nine countries meeting in Snowmass, Colorado, reached a consensus: CFCs are causing the gaps in the ozone layer. _____

12. The leader of the Taliban in Afghanistan issued an edict that girls are not allowed to go to school. _____

13. The doctor noted that more boys than girls are diagnosed with hyperactivity by their teachers. _____

14. Often the starting salary is not commensurate with the experience of the job candidate. _____

15. The premise of the argument was convincing to the audience at the senator's nominating party. _____

16. Geometry is now being introduced to middle-school students. _____

17. Incognito, the king mingled with his subjects so he could hear their honest assessment of him. _____

18. Asymmetrical hemlines were very popular last year. _____

19. The number of scholars at this year's colloquium was double that of last year. _____

20. The sailboat took a circuitous trip out to the island and back. _____

QUIZ YOURSELF   Visit the student companion website at www.cengagebrain.com to check your progress by working with the audio flashcards.

46 RUPT—break

Words that include the word root—RUPT show a *break* of some kind. In the sixteenth century, people used to come together in the market place to buy and sell goods and services. Merchants would set up their businesses on tables or benches. A merchant who ran out of money or incurred too much debt was **bankrupt** [BANK table or bench + RUPT break], and the authorities would *break* his table or bench to symbolize that he was no longer welcome nor had the money to conduct business.

abrupt (ah bruhpt´) [AB off + RUPT break] adjective—ending suddenly. *Her abrupt departure from the party was surprising to the other guests.*

bankrupt (bank ruhpt´) [BANK table or bench + RUPT break] noun—unable to pay outstanding debts. *Christina had no hope of ever repaying her huge debt; she was bankrupt.*

corrupt (kuh ruhpt´) [COR together, with + RUPT break] adjective—guilty of immoral or dishonest practices or actions, often for personal gain. *The corrupt boxer deliberately lost the match.*

disrupt (dis ruhpt´) [DIS apart + RUPT break] verb—(used as a verb with an object) to cause a disturbance or disorder; breaking of order or continuity. *By shouting and blocking speakers from the podium, the conservation society members disrupted the hunters' meeting.*

disruption (dis ruhpt´ shun) [DIS apart + RUPT break] noun—the act of causing a disturbance or a break in order. *Her persistently ringing cell phone caused a disruption during the live performance.*

erupt (ih ruhpt´) [EX out + RUPT break] verb—to explode or burst out, often violently. *The stressed shopper erupted in anger when another shopper cut in the line.*

eruption (ih ruhpt´ shun) [EX out + RUPT break] noun—the act of exploding or bursting out, often violently. *The volcano's eruption caused the islanders to flee.*

interrupt (in tuh ruhpt´) [INTER in + RUPT break] verb—to break the continuity of an action. *Impatient children often interrupt the conversation of others.*

interruption (in tuh ruhp´ shun) [INTER in + RUPT break] noun—the act of breaking the continuity of an action. *Not paying your electric bill will cause an interruption of service.*

rupture (ruhp´ cher) [RUPT break] verb—to break or burst. *The sudden loud explosion caused the soldier's eardrum to rupture.* Or used as a noun—as the act of breaking or bursting. *The flooding was caused by a rupture in the levy system.*

ALSO: abruptly, bankruptcy, corruptible, corruption, incorruptible, uninterrupted

✎ **EXERCISE 1   Fill in the correct RUPT word based on its definition.**

1. _____ the act of causing a disturbance or a break in order
2. _____ guilty of immoral or dishonest practices or actions, often for personal gain
3. _____ ending suddenly
4. _____ to explode or burst out, often violently
5. _____ unable to pay outstanding debts
6. _____ to break the continuity of an action
7. _____ to break or burst

✎ **EXERCISE 2   Fill in the correct RUPT word.**

1. The _____ banker was indicted on several federal charges.
2. Too many _____ (s), such as phone calls and text messages, break my concentration when I am studying.
3. Sam's party came to a(n) _____ end when his parents came home unexpectedly.
4. A fun science project is to add vinegar to baking soda, which causes the chemicals to _____.
5. The broken circuit _____ (ed) the flow of electricity.
6. Because it could not pay back its debts, the company was declared _____ by the court.
7. Numerous loud _____ (s) caused the meeting to break up without completion.
8. The protesters attempted to _____ the opening ceremonies of the Academy Awards.
9. The rising flood waters caused the dam to _____.
10. The geyser Old Faithful can shoot over 8,000 gallons of water during one of its regular _____ (s).

✎ **EXERCISE 3 JOURNAL   Write three sentences in your *vocabulary journal* about disturbances you heard about in the news using RUPT words you have learned. Check with the sentence given in the explanation of each word to make sure you are using the word correctly. For example, *interrupt* is a verb, whereas *interruption* is a noun.**

47 SCRIB, SCRIPT—to write

In Europe during the fifth century, a monk copied a **manuscript**, thus becoming the first European **scribe**. Before long, entire monasteries were devoted to copying scriptural and literary texts. The scribes copied the texts laboriously in black, glossy letters; then other monks illuminated the capital letters with red pigment and gold leaf. Sometimes the making of a single book would occupy many years or even the lifetime of a monk.

ascribe (uh skrīb´) [AD to + SCRIB to write] verb—to attribute. *His parents ascribed his actions to his eagerness to succeed.*

circumscribe (sur´ kum skrīb) [CIRCUM around + SCRIB to write] verb—to limit; to confine. *You are only circumscribed by your attitude; a positive attitude will lead to a positive life.*

conscription (kun skrip´ shun) [CON together + SCRIPT to write] noun—an enforced enrollment or military draft. *Conscription was often necessary to provide a large army.*

inscribe (in skrīb´) [IN in + SCRIB to write] verb—originally, to engrave words in stone; now, to write in, as the dedication of a book. *The author inscribed my copy of her book.*

manuscript (man´ yuh skript) [MANU hand + SCRIPT to write] noun—originally, something written by hand; now, a composition for publication. *He sent his manuscript to the publisher.*

nondescript (non´ di skript) [NON not + SCRIPT to write] adjective—dull; drab; lacking in distinctive qualities. *Even though her outfit was nondescript, she was still the most striking person in the room.*

postscript (pō skript) [POST after + SCRIPT to write] noun—a note written after the main body of a letter (abbreviated P.S.). *P.S. is often used to repeat or include a most important point in a letter or an email.*

prescribe (pri skrīb´) [PRE before + SCRIB to write] verb—to write down a rule beforehand; in medicine, to order a treatment. *The doctor prescribed an antibiotic for the child's sore throat.*

proscribe (pro skrīb´) [PRO before + SCRIB to write] verb—in ancient Rome, to publish the name of one condemned to death; now, to condemn or forbid as harmful. *Some religions proscribe abortion.*

scribe (skrīb) noun—one who copies manuscripts. *In ancient Egypt, scribes were hired to copy important documents.*

script (skript) noun—handwriting; also, the written copy of a play used by actors to learn their lines. *She was studying the script for her part in the play.*

Scripture (skrip´ chur) noun—originally, anything written; now, the Bible. *The library owns the King James version of the Scripture.*

subscribe (sub skrīb´) [SUB under + SCRIB to write] verb—to write one's name on an agreement, as to subscribe to a magazine; also, to support or give approval to an idea. *Congress subscribed to the foreign policy of the president.*

transcribe (tran skrīb´) [TRANS over + SCRIB to write] verb—to write over again, as to transcribe notes. *After the class, the student transcribed her messy notes to ones that were legible.*

ALSO: describe, description, descriptive, prescription, prescriptive, scribble, subscription, transcript

✎ **EXERCISE 1   Write the SCRIB, SCRIPT word next to its definition.**

1. _____ military draft
2. _____ to attribute
3. _____ composition for publication
4. _____ the Bible
5. _____ a note written after the main body of a letter
6. _____ to write in
7. _____ condemn or forbid as harmful

✎ **EXERCISE 2   Write the appropriate SCRIB, SCRIPT word.**

1. They will probably _____ the failure of their plan to lack of funds.

2. His clothes were always _____ and monotone in color.

3. It's wise to _____ one's class notes immediately after taking them.

4. During times of peace, _____ is unnecessary.

5. Do you _____ to new ideas?

6. The laws _____ racial discrimination in employment and housing.

7. The new penny is _____ (ed) with a flower.

8. Most writers no longer handwrite their _____ (s) since the advent of computers.

9. Part of her theater class focused on _____ writing.

10. The minister crafts each sermon to focus on a different part of the _____.

11. Did the doctor _____ that new medicine for your ailment?

12. Since the advent of the printing press, we no longer use _____ to copy biblical texts.

13. Helen Keller never felt _____ by her disabilities; rather she used them to her advantage.

14. Many times the _____ is I love you!

48 SED, SID, SESS—to sit

If you have a **sedentary** job, you probably *sit* at a desk all day. If you work **assiduously**, you literally *sit* at your work until it is finished. And if you have an **insidious** habit, it is one that does not seem very bad at first but *sits* in wait for you, ready to become more and more harmful.

assess (uh ses´) [AD to + SESS to sit] verb—to estimate the value of property for taxation; to estimate a situation or an event. *Their property was assessed at a higher rate than they thought after purchasing the fixer upper.*

assessor (uh ses´ ur) [AD to + SESS to sit] noun—an official who assesses property for taxation. *They were waiting for the assessor to evaluate their new home.*

assiduous (uh sij´ O us) adjective—sitting at something until it is finished; persistent. *The new clerk was assiduous in performing all his duties.*

insidious (in sid´ ē us) [IN in + SID to sit] adjective—sitting in wait for; treacherous, more dangerous than seems evident. *Malaria is an insidious disease, remaining in the body ready to strike again and again.*

obsess (ub ses´) [OB against + SESS to sit] verb—to preoccupy the mind abnormally. *He was obsessed with the fear of failure.*

obsession (ub sesh´ un) [OB against + SESS to sit] noun—a persistent idea, desire, or emotion that cannot be got rid of by reasoning. *Her desire to act in movies had become an obsession.*

preside (pri zīd´) [PRE before + SID to sit] verb—to sit before a meeting to conduct it. *The vice president had to preside in the president's absence.*

president (prez´ ud unt) [PRE before + SID to sit] noun—one who sits before a group as its head. *We waited for the president to state his views.* (The "p" in president is capitalized when used as a proper noun: President Obama.)

sedative (sed´ uh tiv) noun—a medicine that calms nervousness or excitement. *The doctor prescribed a sedative so that her patient could get some rest.*

sedentary (sed´ n ter ē) adjective—requiring much sitting. *Because he had a sedentary job, he didn't get enough exercise.*

sediment (sed´ uh munt) noun—material that sits at the bottom of a liquid, as the sediment in a stream. *We noted the sediment in the bottom of the glass.*

session (sesh´ un) noun—the sitting together of a group. *School is in session now.*

siege (sēj) noun—a prolonged attack, as of war or illness. *She had a siege of flu that lasted all winter. The Siege of Stalingrad changed the outcome of World War II.*

subside (sub sīd´) [SUB under + SID to sit] verb—to sink to a lower level; to settle down. *After midnight, the noise subsided.*

subsidiary (sub sid´ ē er ē) [SUB under + SID to sit] adjective—serving to assist or supplement; subordinate. *The large record company had several subsidiary labels.*

subsidy (sub´ suh dē) [SUB under + SID to sit] noun—government financial support. *When corn prices were low, the farmers received a subsidy.*

supersede (sO pur sēd´) [SUPER above + SED to sit] verb—to take the place of; to displace. *Solar heating is superseding other forms of heating in many areas.*

ALSO: dissident, reside, residue, sedan

✎ **EXERCISE 1   Write the appropriate SED, SID, SESS word.**

1. A(n) _____ occupation has never appealed to her because she doesn't like to sit still.

2. Nevertheless, she was a(n) _____ worker, doing the job to the best of her ability.

3. The government's _____ to the auto industry was not enough to save several auto companies.

4. The chemicals had a(n) _____ effect on the stream, the real damage not showing up for months.

5. The complaints of the environmentalists about the pollution did not _____ when the election was over.

6. The computer has _____ (ed) the typewriter.

7. Having everything immaculate is a(n) _____ with her.

8. Many companies' _____ branches are located overseas, where labor is cheaper.

9. Becoming _____ (ed) with a desire to win, he thought of nothing else.

10. What he has done for the school is so important that it would be difficult to _____ its value.

11. The county _____ evaluated their home's value for tax purposes.

12. During the Middle Ages, enemies laid _____ against each other by fighting continuous battles.

13. Ellen's doctor prescribed a _____ after the traumatic accident.

14. All U.S. presidents _____ over the military.

15. The instructor assured us that each _____ of class was sure to be informative.

16. The _____ at the bottom of the lake squished between our toes.

17. The _____ of the bank started out as a teller and worked his way up.

✎ **EXERCISE 2 JOURNAL   In your *vocabulary journal*, write several sentences about a writing project you've done. Use as many RUPT, SCRIB, SCRIPT, and SED, SID, SESS words as possible.**

49 SPEC, SPIC, SPECT—to look

In ancient Rome, certain men were appointed to *look* at the flight of birds for omens or signs. The kind of birds, their position in the sky, and the direction of their flight determined whether the time was **auspicious** [AVI bird + SPIC to look] for any new undertaking. **Auspicious** came to mean "full of good omens," and today we still speak of an auspicious time to ask a favor or to suggest a new policy.

aspect (as´ pekt) [AD to + SPECT to look] noun—the way something looks from a certain point of view. *He was concerned about another aspect of the case.*

auspicious (aw spish´ us) [AVI bird + SPIC to look] adjective—promising good luck; favorable. *It was an auspicious time to ask for a raise because the company's revenues were very profitable.*

circumspect (sur´ kum spekt) [CIRCUM around + SPEC to look] adjective—cautious; careful to consider possible consequences. *She was circumspect in answering the police officer's questions; she knew her first amendment rights.*

conspicuous (kun spik´ yuh wus) [CON (intensive) + SPIC to look] adjective—easy to notice (look at); obvious. *Her late arrival made her conspicuous.*

introspection (in truh spek´ shun) [INTRO within + SPECT to look] noun—a looking within one's own mind. *Introspection was valuable in helping her solve some of her problems.*

perspective (pur spek´ tiv) [PER through + SPECT to look] noun—the ability to look at things in their true relationship; point of view. *Whether you consider the difficulty insurmountable depends on your perspective.*

perspicacious (per spi kā´ shus) [PER through + SPIC to look] adjective—having the ability to look through something and understand it; perceptive. *In dealing with individual employee problems, he was exceptionally perspicacious.*

prospect (prah´ spekt) [PRO forward + SPECT to look] noun—a looking forward; the outlook for something, as a prospect for a good crop. *The prospect for lower taxes is slim.*

respect (ri spekt´) [RE again + SPECT to look] noun—to look on with regard or esteem. *We have the greatest respect for our leader.*

retrospect (ret´ ruh spekt) [RETRO backward + SPECT to look] noun—a looking backward. *In retrospect, his life did not seem so unhappy.*

specious (spē´ shus) adjective—looking good or desirable on first sight but actually not so once looking at its validity. *It was hard not to be taken in by the specious advertising for the baldness remedy.*

specter (spec´tur) noun—a mental image that looks real; a ghost; any object of fear or dread. *Her father was troubled by the specter of unemployment.*

spectrum (spek´ trum) noun—a series of colored bands seen when light passes through a prism. *All the colors of the spectrum were included in her painting.* Also, a broad range of ideas or activities. *His interests included the entire spectrum of the arts.*

speculate (spek´ yuh lāt) verb—to reflect on or ponder. *The candidate speculated on his chances of winning.*

ALSO: despicable, expect, inauspicious, inspect, introspective, perspicacity, prospective, prospector, prospectus, respectable, retrospection, species, specific, specimen, spectacle, spectacles, spectacular, spectator, suspect, suspicious

✎ **EXERCISE 1   Write the appropriate SPEC, SPIC, SPECT word.**

1. The failure of the first project was not a(n) _____ start for the coming year.

2. The salesperson could see the problem from the customer's _____.

3. She enjoyed living those years again in _____.

4. He examined his motives in a moment of quiet _____.

5. She was _____ when giving feedback to her boss.

6. The professor was unusually _____ in analyzing the problems of the students.

7. The _____ advertising made the car deal looked like a giveaway; it was too good to be true.

8. One experiences the entire _____ of emotions watching that play.

9. The _____ of failure haunted her.

10. The golf pro wouldn't _____ on the outcome of the U.S. Open.

11. The _____ of all that paperwork put him in a bad mood.

12. The residents of the retirement home are involved in all _____ (s) of their daily living.

13. Her neon-colored tie-dyed dress was _____ in the crowd of conservative dressers.

14. I _____ the advice from my professors.

✎ **EXERCISE 2 REVIEW   Match each word with its definition.**

A. protuberant	**D.** apathy	**G.** metamorphosis	**I.** malaise
B. interrupt	**E.** loquacious	**H.** precocious	**J.** epigram
C. monarchy	**F.** perfidious		

1. _____ government with one hereditary ruler

2. _____ bulging

3. _____ break in or bust up

4. _____ talkative

5. _____ lack of feeling; indifference

6. _____ deceiving through pretense of faith; treacherous

7. _____ the ability to change form or shape

8. _____ vague feeling of illness or depression

9. _____ prematurely developed

10. _____ writing on any subject; short witty saying

50 SUB—under

Prisoners in Roman times were forced to crawl *under* a yoke (like the yoke put on oxen) formed from three spears, thus showing that from that time forward they were the subjects of their conquerors. They were brought *under* (SUB) the yoke (JUGUM) or **subjugated**. We still use the word **subjugate** today to mean subdue or make **subservient**.

Many SUB words are easy to understand when we know that SUB means *under*: **subcommittee, subconscious, subcontractor, subculture, subnormal, substandard**, and **subway**. But SUB can also help clarify the meaning of some less common words such as **subliminal** and **subsume**. **Sub rosa** literally means "under the rose," from an ancient custom of hanging a rose over the council table to indicate that all present were sworn to secrecy. Now it means in confidence or in secrecy.

subject (accent on last syllable) (sub jekt´) [SUB under + JECT to throw] verb—to submit to the authority of, as to subject oneself to a strict diet. *She learned to subject herself to the office routine.* (There is also, of course, **subject** with the accent on the first syllable. This is the noun form. *Her favorite subject is math.*)

subjugate (sub´ juh gāt) [SUB under + JUGUM a yoke] verb—to conquer. *The invaders subjugated the primitive tribe.*

subliminal (sub lim´ uh nul) [SUB under + LIMIN threshold] adjective—below the threshold of conscious perception. *The popcorn ad flashed on the theater screen too briefly to be seen consciously, but it had a subliminal effect—people immediately started going to the lobby for popcorn.*

submerge (sub murj´) [SUB under + MERG to plunge] adjective or verb—to plunge under water. *I learned to swim a few strokes when completely submerged. Because I didn't swim, I was afraid to submerge my body into the lake.*

subpoena (suh pē nuh) [SUB under + POENA penalty (the first two words of the order)] noun—a legal order requiring a person to appear in court to give testimony. *She received a subpoena to appear in court the next week.*

sub rosa (sub ro´ zuh) [SUB under + ROS rose] noun—in confidence; in secrecy. *President Obama acted sub rosa when ordering Navy Seals to capture and kill Osama Bin Laden.*

subservient (sub sur´ vē unt) [SUB under + SERV to serve] adjective—serving under someone; submissive, as a servant might be. *His attitude toward his superiors was always subservient.*

subsistence (sub sis´ tunts) noun—literally under existence; the barest means to sustain life. *They had barely enough food for subsistence.*

subsume (sub sOm´) [SUB under + SUM to take] verb—to include under a more general category. *The three minor rules are subsumed under the major one.*

subterfuge (sub´ tur fyOj) [SUB under + FUG to flee] noun—an action used to avoid an unpleasant situation. *By using the subterfuge of having to work overtime, he avoided going to the meeting.*

subterranean (sub tuh ra´ nē un) [SUB under + TERR earth] adjective—under the surface of the Earth. *Subterranean remains of an early civilization were found on the island.*

subversive (sub vur´ siv) [SUB under + VERS to turn] adjective—tending to undermine or overthrow. *The government was threatened by subversive groups.*

ALSO: subcutaneous, subjective, submarine, submit, subordinate, subscribe, subsequent, subside, subsidy, subtle, suburb, suffuse, surreptitious

✏ EXERCISE 1   Match the SUB word with its definition.

A. subjugate   **C.** subpoena   **E.** subterfuge
B. subliminal   **D.** sub rosa   **F.** subversive

1. _____ undermine or overthrow
2. _____ legal order to appear in court
3. _____ to conquer
4. _____ action used to avoid an unpleasant situation
5. _____ in confidence; secrecy
6. _____ below the threshold of conscious perception

✏ EXERCISE 2   Write the appropriate SUB word.

1. He was completely _____ by the giant wave.
2. The prison inmates were _____ to strict rules.
3. With such a low-paying job, he and his family lived at a _____ level.
4. The dictator was trying to quell the _____ forces in the country.
5. She thought of a clever _____ to get out of doing the job.
6. He was so _____ that he never objected to his supervisor's unreasonable demands.
7. The superpower was trying to _____ all the small nations around it.
8. A person can be influenced not only in conscious ways but also in _____ ways.
9. All his arguments can be _____ in a summarized document.
10. The driver of the other car received a _____ to appear in court as a witness.
11. Bats flew out of the _____ cave.
12. Unwilling to have his remarks published, the dean asked that they be considered _____.

EXTRA PRACTICE A, AN—SUB

EXERCISE 1 Use the following words to complete the sentences below.

intercede   generic   benediction   benevolent   efface

hyperglycemia   monoliths   genocide   kilometers   malevolent

1. She tried to _____ from her mind the scene that had just taken place.
2. _____ affects one out of every four adults in the United States.
3. At the close of the service, the minister pronounced the _____.
4. Interfering with a tribe's way of gathering food can be a form of _____.
5. We marveled at how the ancients had moved the _____ at Stonehenge.
6. She always tried to buy _____ food products because they are usually less expensive than brand-name products.
7. The speaker was aware of the _____ glances of his opponents.
8. When we drove in Canada, we had to think in _____ rather than in miles.
9. Her handling of the problem was so _____ that everyone was grateful.
10. The mother will _____ on her child's behalf.

EXERCISE 2 Match the word with its definition.

1. _____ malfeasance
2. _____ anthropology
3. _____ soliloquy
4. _____ engender
5. _____ perfidious

A. speaking alone to oneself as in a drama

B. deceiving through pretense of faith; treacherous

C. wrongdoing, especially by a public official

D. to give birth to; to develop; to bring forth

E. the study of the physical, social, cultural development, and behavior of human beings

EXERCISE 3 Underline the word(s) that you have studied so far and provide the meaning(s). Check in the Word Index for any words you don't remember.

1. The ancient Roman belief in many gods is called pantheism. _____

2. The proponents of recycling are trying to bring it to the town. _____

3. When her appendix ruptured, she had emergency surgery. _____

4. The prospectus for the new housing development made us want to move there. _____

5. The demon in her dream was amorphous. _____

6. The Renaissance period brought forth a new period of enlightenment. _____

7. The captain had set a precedent of fair play that his teammates now followed. _____

8. The loquacious student was asked to listen to others recite the soliloquy. _____ and _____

9. Because she was ambidextrous, she played golf with her left hand and tennis with her right. _____

10. Sharon showed empathy to Charles when he separated from his partner. _____

11. The child's fear of the dark has become a phobia. _____

12. No one has ever doubted the credibility of our governor. _____

13. The woman accused in the Salem Witch trials refused to recant. _____

14. The witches put a malediction on Macbeth. _____

15. After a very long run, I often feel enervated. _____

16. Living in Hawaii offers a chance to see a volcanic eruption with lava flows pouring to the ocean. _____

17. The maladroit server disrupted the ceremony when he dropped all the wine glasses. _____ and _____

18. No one can trust the perfidious, corrupt politician after the news broke of his malfeasance. _____ , _____ and _____

QUIZ YOURSELF Visit the student companion website at www.cengagebrain.com to check your progress by working with the audio flashcards.

51 SUPER—above, over

How do you describe people who raise their eyebrows and look down on others in a haughty way? Two roots—SUPER *above* and CILIUM *eyelid*—combined to form the Latin word *supercilium* meaning eyebrow. Eventually, anyone who raised their eyebrows in a haughty way came to be called a **supercilious** person, a raised-eyebrows person.

insuperable (in sO´ pur uh bul) [IN not + SUPER over] adjective—not capable of being overcome. *His height was an insuperable barrier to his becoming a jockey.*

soprano (su pran´ ō) noun—one having a voice range above other voices. *Her soprano solo was the highlight of the concert.*

supercilious (sO pur sil´ e us) [SUPER above + CILIUM eyelid] adjective—eyebrows raised in a haughty, conceited way. *She cast a supercilious glance at her sister who had dared to disagree with her.*

superfluous (su pur´ fO wus) [SUPER over + FLU to flow] adjective—overflowing what is needed; extra. *The essay was full of superfluous words.*

superimpose (sO pur im poz´) noun—to lay something over something else. *In the anatomy book, superimposed diagrams show the circulatory, muscular, and skeletal systems in connection to one another.*

supernumerary (sO pur nO´ muh rer ē) [SUPER above + NUMER number] noun—someone in excess of (above) the number required; an extra. *Because she was given no work to do, she felt like a supernumerary.* Also, a performer in the theater without a speaking part; an extra in a scene. *He was a supernumerary in the mob scene of the movie.*

supersonic (sO pur son´ ik) [SUPER above + SON sound] adjective—above the speed of sound. *Supersonic planes cause the sound known as sonic boom.*

superstition (sO pur stish´ un) [SUPER above + STA to stand] noun—a belief that is inconsistent with the known laws of science. *Believing that the number 13 is unlucky is a superstition.*

surplus (sur´ plus) [SUPER above + PLUS more] noun—above what is needed. *With over fifty, we have a surplus of volunteers.*

ALSO: supersede, superb, superior, superabundant, superannuated, superhuman, superintend, supernatural, supersede, supervise, supervisor, supreme

EXERCISE 1   Which SUPER word names or describes the following?

1. _____ above the speed of sound
2. _____ above what is needed
3. _____ to lay something over something else
4. _____ incapable of being overcome
5. _____ haughty
6. _____ someone in excess of what is required
7. _____ extra; overflowing of what is needed

✎ EXERCISE 2 Fill in the correct SUPER word.

1. My grandfather believed every _____, especially about breaking mirrors causing bad luck.

2. The _____ singer in our chorus has a light, pretty voice.

3. Alexis's _____ comments added an extra hour to the meeting.

4. The fledging actor was happy just to get the _____ role in the movie.

5. The restaurant donated the _____ food to the poor.

6. The athlete overcame _____ odds to compete after his ankle injury.

7. _____ is a sophisticated way to express conceit.

✎ EXERCISE 3 REVIEW Underline the appropriate word.

1. Morse code is an (anachronistic, antithesis) in the digital age.

2. Many new relationships bring up feelings of (philanthropy, euphoria) and (ambivalence, remission) simultaneously.

3. "Lots of kids flunked" is a (disconsolate, colloquial) expression for "many students failed."

4. Having a college-level vocabulary is a (prerequisite, sub rosa) for excellent reading comprehension.

5. A (prescriptive, perfidious) argument makes claims about how the world should operate.

✎ EXERCISE 4 REVIEW As a review of the words you've been studying, read this paragraph. How many of the ten underlined words do you know without looking them up? Add any you are unsure of to your WORD LIST.

A town meeting was called to consider a lumber company's proposal to cut trees in a town-owned woodland. The <u>proponents</u> of the plan claimed it would create jobs and bring <u>unprecedented</u> wealth to the town, which was in <u>chronic</u> economic depression. They said that those trying to <u>circumvent</u> the plan were asking for the <u>demise</u> of the community. Those interested in <u>ecology</u>, on the other hand, said that the natural beauty of the area would be spoiled and that several <u>endemic</u> plants might become extinct. It isn't possible, they said, to <u>equate</u> financial gain with the good life. The problem seemed <u>insuperable</u> because after three hours of discussion, no <u>consensus</u> was reached.

52 SYN, SYM, SYL—together, with

Among the ancient Greeks, a **symposium** was a *drinking together* party [SYM together + POS to drink], especially after a banquet. Through the years, the meaning has changed until today a symposium is no longer a drinking party but a meeting or conference at which several speakers come *together* to deliver opinions on a certain topic.

In preceding pages, we have seen that the root SYN, SYM, SYL means *together* in such words as **symmetrical**, **sympathy**, **symphony**, and **synchronize**. Whether the word will begin with SYN, SYM, or SYL often depends on what letter follows. For instance, it would be difficult to pronounce SYNmetrical; therefore, SYN becomes SYM. For more about how a root may change one of its letters for easier pronunciation, see page 5.

syllogism (sil´ uh jiz um) [SYL together + LOG word] noun—a form of argument or reasoning consisting of two statements and a conclusion drawn from them. *Here is an example of a syllogism: All mammals are warm-blooded; whales are mammals; therefore, whales are warm-blooded.*

symbol (sim´ bul) [SYM together + BOL to throw] noun—as a comparison; something that represents something else. *Diamonds are a symbol of wealth.*

symposium (sim po´ zee um) [SYM together + POS to drink] noun—a meeting at which several speakers deliver opinions on a certain topic. *A symposium on the use of national parks was held in Washington, D.C.*

synagogue (sin´ u gahg) [SYN together + AGOG to lead] noun—a place where Jews come together for worship; also called a temple. *The oldest synagogue in the United States, Touro Synagogue, is in Newport, Rhode Island.*

syndrome (sin´ drōm) [SYN together + DROM to run] noun—a group of symptoms that run together and indicate a specific disease or condition. *He had the usual flu syndrome: sore throat, headache, and aching muscles.*

synergistic (sin ur jis´ tik) [SYN together + ERG work] adjective—working together, as when the joint action of two or more things or people increases the effectiveness of each. *Certain drugs are synergistic when taken together. The two playwrights had a synergistic relationship, each working more effectively when they worked together.*

synopsis (su nahp´ sus) [SYN together + OP sight] noun—a brief general summary. *Before beginning our study of the novel, we read a synopsis of it.*

syntax (sin´ tax) [SYN together + TAX arrangement] noun—the way words are arranged together to form sentences. *Because English was a second language for her, she often had trouble with syntax.*

synthesis (sin´ thuh sis) [SYN together + THES to put] noun—the combining of separate elements into a whole. *The chemistry experiment calls for the synthesis of hydrogen and oxygen to make water.*

ALSO: asymmetric, photosynthesis, symbiosis, symbiotic, symmetrical, sympathy, symphony, synchronize, synergy, synod, synonym, synthetic

EXERCISE 1   Write the appropriate SYN, SYM, SYL word.

1. The final motion was a _____ of all their ideas.

2. Six speakers were scheduled for the _____ on air pollution.

3. The diagnosis was simple because the child had the typical chickenpox _____.

4. Because he had never paid any attention to grammar in high school, he now had difficulty using correct _____ in his writing.

5. Learning the correct form for a _____ helped her to think logically.

6. She and her husband had a _____ relationship, each working better on the project when they worked together.

7. In an early chapter of *The Grapes of Wrath,* John Steinbeck uses a turtle as a _____ of the migrants.

8. Jews pray in a _____, Muslims pray in a mosque, Christians pray in a church, and Hindus pray in a temple.

9. The _____ of chemicals made a large explosion, injuring two laboratory workers.

EXERCISE 2 REVIEW   Match the word to its definition.

1. _____ superfluous

2. _____ perspicacious

3. _____ assiduous

4. _____ proscribe

5. _____ recalcitrant

A. persistent

B. condemn or forbid as harmful

C. stubbornly rebellious

D. overflowing what is needed; extra

E. having the ability to look through something and understand it; perceptive

EXERCISE 3 JOURNAL   Write several sentences in your *vocabulary journal* about a symposium you have attended using words from the roots SUPER, and SYN, SYM, SYL. Pick words you had trouble remembering.

✎ **EXERCISE 4**   **Give the meaning of each root and a word in which it is found.**

ROOT	MEANING	WORD
1. A, AN		
2. AMBI, AMPHI		
3. ANN, ENN		
4. ANTE		
5. ANTHROP		
6. ANTI		
7. AUTO		
8. BENE		
9. BIO		
10. BI		
11. CEDE, CEED		
12. CHRON		
13. CIRCUM		
14. COGNI, GNOS		
15. COM, CON, COL, COR		
16. CRED		
17. CUR		
18. DEM		
19. DICT		
20. DIS, DI, DIF		
21. EQU		
22. EU		
23. EX, ES, E		
24. FID		
25. GEN		

ROOT	MEANING	WORD
26. GRAPH, GRAM		
27. HYPER		
28. LOG		
29. -LOGY		
30. LOQU, LOC		
31. MAL		
32. METER, METR		
33. MIT, MIS, MISS		
34. MONO		
35. MORPH		
36. PAN		
37. PATH		
38. PED		
39. PHIL		
40. PHOB		
41. PHON		
42. POST		
43. PRE		
44. PRO		
45. RE		
46. RUPT		
47. SCRIB, SCRIPT		
48. SED, SID, SESS		
49. SPEC, SPIC, SPECT		
50. SUB		
51. SUPER		
52. SYN, SYM, SYL		

53 TAIN, TEN, TIN—to hold

Once you know that the root TAIN, TEN, TIN means to *hold*, you can see its meaning in many words. A **container** [CON together + TAIN to hold] is used to *hold* anything from a small marble collection to large cargo that is shipped around the world. A **tenant** is a person who *holds* land by title or lease. And if you get **detention**, you are *held* in custody. The first recorded use of **detain** was in 1570 when Mary Queen of Scots was *held* captive in English prisons by her English cousin, Queen Elizabeth I.

abstain (ab´ stain) [AB away + TAIN hold] verb—to refrain deliberately from an action or practice by one's own choice. *If you can abstain from smoking until you are twenty-one, you probably will never start.*

contents (kon´ tent) [CON together + TENT hold] noun—the things that are inside a container. *She shook the box to try to figure out its contents.*

entertain (en´ ter tain) [ENT inner + TAIN to hold] verb—to hold, keep, or maintain in the mind. *Knowing the area well, he entertained the idea of starting a business guiding tourists to the local sites.*

detain (de tay´ n) [DE away + TAIN to hold] verb—to hold back or keep in. *We were detained at the country's border while the guard checked our passports.*

obstinate (ob´ stin ate) adjective—holding to an opinion, purpose, or course in spite of reason, arguments, or persuasion. *Journalist Katherine Whitehorn wrote the humorous lines, "I am firm. You are obstinate. He is a pig-headed fool."*

pertain (per´ tayn) [PER through + TAIN hold] verb—to belong to as a part, member, accessory, or product. *Critical thinking, as it pertains to learning, involves understanding, analysis, and evaluation.*

retentive (re ten´ tive) [RE again + TEN hold] adjective—holding onto something easily, such as retentive soil or a retentive memory. *A retentive memory is good, but sometimes the ability to forget is just as important.*

sustain (suhs tayn) [SUS up + TAIN hold] verb—to hold up, give support or relief. *Growing their own food will sustain them during hard times.*

tenacious (ten´ a shus) adjective—persistent in maintaining or holding onto something, such as a point of view. *Dr. Martin Luther King Jr. was a tenacious advocate of civil rights.*

tenure (ten´ yure) noun—the act, right, manner, or term of holding something (as a landed property, a position, or an office), especially a status granted after a trial period to a teacher that gives protection from summary dismissal. *Between her positive teaching evaluations and numerous publications, she was certain to be granted tenure at the college.*

ALSO: contain, detainee, detention, incontinent, obtain, retain, retention, tenable, tenant, tenet

✎ **EXERCISE 1   Write the appropriate TAIN, TEN, TIN word.**

1. The baby's _____ grip on his big brother's finger made him laugh.

2. Good water-_____ soil, rich in organic matter, is the best type for a vegetable garden.

3. As a vegetarian, she eats fruits and vegetables but _____ (s) from meat.

4. Her _____ as the chairperson will end in 2017.

5. A fierce fight arose when the police officers attempted to _____ the offenders.

6. The _____ of the safe-deposit box are known only to the holder of the box.

7. My _____ character has propelled me to successfully meet most challenges.

8. One way to _____ the gain in your vocabulary is to use your new words regularly.

9. The audience is asked to refrain from making comments that do not _____ to the discussion topic.

10. Her convivial company _____ (s) when I am filled with malaise.

✎ **EXERCISE 2   Which TAIN, TEN, TIN word names or describes the following?**

1. _____ to hold back or keep in

2. _____ holding to an opinion, purpose or course in spite of reason

3. _____ to belong to as a part, member, accessory or product

4. _____ holding onto something easily

5. _____ persistent in maintaining or holding onto something

✎ **EXERCISE 3 JOURNAL   In your *vocabulary journal*, write several sentences about your goals for the future using as many SUB and TAIN, TEN, TIN words as possible. Remember, if you use a word three times, it is yours.**

If you are driving along a little-traveled mountain road, you will certainly understand the meaning of **tortuous**. It comes from the root TORT *to twist* and means full of *twists* and turns. You can speak of a tortuous road, a tortuous path through the woods, a tortuous climb down a mountain, a tortuous career with advances and reverses all along the way, or tortuous arguments that wander all over rather than moving directly toward a goal. Tortuous may also mean morally *twisted*, deceitful, not straightforward. Tortuous explanations may *twist* the truth, and tortuous deals may be *twisted* or crooked.

Tortuous must not be confused with **torturous**, which is related to torture and means inflicting physical or mental pain.

contortionist (kun tawr´ shun ist) [CON together + TORT to twist] noun—an acrobat who can twist the body and limbs into extraordinary positions. *At the circus, the children watched an expert contortionist perform.*

distort (dis tawrt´) [DIS away + TORT to twist] verb—to twist from the true meaning, as to distort the facts. *The passenger's description of the accident distorted the facts.*

extort (ik stawrt´) [EX out + TORT to twist] verb—to obtain by violence or threat. *They tried to extort money by blackmail.*

retort (ri tawrt´) [RE back + TORT to twist] verb—a reply to an insult or a criticism. *His retort to her criticism was shattering.*

torment (tawr ment´) verb—to annoy. *The mosquitoes tormented us as we tried to sleep in our tent in the woods.*

tort (tawrt) noun—a wrongful act, injury, or damage for which a civil suit can be brought for damages. *If a person breaks a shop window, that person has committed a tort against the shop owner.*

tortuous (tawrch´ uh wus) adjective—full of twists and turns. *We drove on Lombard Street in San Francisco, the most crooked street in the world; it was fun and tortuous.* Also, not straightforward; deceitful. *Our mayor was tortuous; I knew we couldn't trust her.*

torture (tawr´ chur) noun—any severe physical or mental pain. *The Human Rights Commission states the "waterboarding prisoners of war is a form of torture."*

torturous (tawrch´ uh rus) adjective—inflicting physical or mental pain. *The prisoner had to endure torturous questioning about his role in the attacks of 9/11/2001.*

ALSO: contortion, torch, torque, torsion, tortoise

✎ **EXERCISE 1   Write the appropriate TORT word.**

1. The mobster tried to _____ money in exchange for "protection."

2. The defense attorney's _____ to the prosecutor convinced the jury of his client's innocence.

3. The audience was amazed at the acrobatic performance of the _____.

4. Emphasizing unimportant details, the student tried to _____ the fact that she plagiarized her term paper.

5. Hydroplaning while driving can be _____ with the twists and turns of skidding on the wet road.

6. Having all her wisdom teeth pulled was _____.

7. The civil suit regarding that _____ was settled out of court.

✎ **EXERCISE 2 REVIEW   Underline the appropriate word.**

1. The (posterior, anterior) legs of an animal are its front legs.

2. The (Preamble, missive) to the Constitution begins with the words "We the people of the United States, in order to form a more perfect Union. . . ."

3. The small nation refused to be (subjugated, sub rosa) by its powerful neighbor.

4. Although she did not appear ill, her friends knew she was suffering from an (insidious, sedimentary) disease.

5. By a clever (subterfuge, subpoena) he avoided taking part in the debate.

6. Her (proclivity, promontory) toward revealing trade secrets cost Sami her job.

7. The (recluse, referee) refused to leave his monastery.

8. The speaker claimed that tax reform would be a (panacea, panoply) for all the ills of the country.

9. She was (apathetic, pathetic) when she heard that she had been fired; she really didn't care.

10. Always a (sedate, ebullient) person, she kicked off her shoes and sat in front of her computer for hours.

11. The (synergy, symbiosis) of the committee resulted in great accomplishments.

12. (Precedent, Antecedent) was set once the tort was entered into law allowing for same-sex marriage in Vermont.

13. Most of the work in that company is done not in the main office but in the (subsidiary, subsidy) offices.

14. There is a strong (correlation, commotion) between persistence to study and cognitive strengths in successful college students' grade point averages.

15. Deductive and inductive reasoning use (syllogism, syntax) to arrive at logical conclusions.

16. (Metacognition, Metamorphosis) is an important skill when learning (etymology, entomology) of words.

17. The nanny was moved to tears by the children's (obstinate, profuse) behavior.

18. The volcano (disrupted, erupted), (emitting, omitting) lava.

55 VER—true

If you doubt someone's **veracity**, you doubt that person's *truthfulness*. If you speak of a **veritable** downpour of rain, you mean that it was *truly* a downpour. To **verify** something is to prove that it is *true*. When jury members give a **verdict** [VER true + DICT to speak], they are literally speaking the *truth*. Even the little word **very** comes from VER and means *truly*.

veracious (vuh ra´ shus) adjective—truthful; accurate. *The newspaper gave a veracious account of the incident.*

veracity (vuh ras´ uh tē) noun—truthfulness. *Having never told a lie in her dealings with others, her veracity is without question.*

verdict (vur´ dikt) [VER true + DICT to speak] noun—the decision of a jury. *The jury gave its verdict of not guilty.*

verifiable (ver´ uh fī uh bul) adjective—capable of being proved true. *None of his statements were verifiable.*

verification (ver ruh fuh ka´ shun) noun—establishment of the truth. *Before cashing the check, the clerk asked for verification of the customer's identity.*

verify (ver´ u fī) verb—to prove something is true. *I can verify all the figures in my account.*

verily (ver´ uh lē) adverb—an archaic word meaning truly. *"He had verily no command of his reason," wrote George Meredith in his novel The Egoist.*

veritable (ver´ uh tuh bul) adjective—true; actual. *Mother Teresa was a veritable good samaritan.*

verity (ver´ uh tē) noun—a statement, principle, or belief that is considered to be established truth, as religious verities. *"Love your neighbor as yourself" is a verity to live by.*

very (ver´ē) adverb—truly, absolutely. *The restaurant is in the very heart of the city.*

ALSO: aver, verisimilitude

✎ EXERCISE 1   Write the VER word that matches its definition.

1. _____ truthful; accurate
2. _____ capable of being proved true
3. _____ an archaic word meaning truly
4. _____ a statement, principle, or belief that is considered to be establish truth
5. _____ truthfulness
6. _____ establishment of the truth
7. _____ to prove something is true
8. _____ truly, absolutely
9. _____ the decision of the jury
10. _____ true; actual

EXERCISE 2 **Write the appropriate VER word.**

1. With her amazing knowledge of facts, she's a _____ encyclopedia.

2. He'd never lie to you; you can depend on his _____.

3. I was careful to _____ each fact before presenting it.

4. The travel agent asked for _____ of the child's age.

5. You can count on her to give a _____ report of the trial because she always tells the truth.

6. Little _____ evidence could be obtained about the accident because there had been no witnesses.

7. He was now questioning some of the _____ he had always accepted in his youth.

8. The formal old way to say truly, _____, is not used in our language today.

9. Jurors must reach a unanimous _____ in murder trials.

10. At only four feet tall, my grandmother is _____ short.

EXERCISE 3 JOURNAL **Write several sentences in your *vocabulary journal* using words from the roots TORT and VER. Pick words you had trouble remembering.**

EXERCISE 1 Underline the appropriate word.

1. Their (assiduous, insidious) tactics misled their clients.

2. My sister has a (phobic, endemic) dread of air travel.

3. The dean suspected that there were (subversive, subsistence) activities going on in the dorms.

4. Because of his (xenophobia, photophobia), he had to avoid strong sunlight.

5. The police (prescribed, ascribed) the accident to drunken driving.

6. The (veracity, verdict) of the witness was never questioned.

7. The clear skies (preclude, presage) a pleasant day.

8. The contestant was (assessed, obsessed) with a desire to succeed.

9. The view from the (promontory, proclivity) was inspiring.

10. Judaism is the first religion to practice (monotheism, pantheism).

11. The (extortionist, contortionist) blackmailed the victim for money.

12. Our Supreme Court (proscribes, transcribes) our harmful laws.

13. The importance of using (syllogisms, synopsizes) in formal logic is paramount.

14. The wordy essay used (superfluous, supercilious) examples to support the thesis.

15. The best way to understand one's self is to become (introspective, despicable).

16. The (barometer, metronome) helped the piano student keep the beat of the music.

17. The doctor prescribed an (antagonist, antibiotic) but the child refused to swallow it.

18. She was moved to tears by the (pathos, apathy) in the story.

EXERCISE 2 Using the following words, fill in the blanks in the paragraph so that it makes sense. After you check your answers, reread the paragraph and see how satisfying it is to read a paragraph in which you are sure of all the words.

assessor	recession	remit
subsidy	assess	revise

When the _____ came to _____ our home, we were hoping with the

_____ that he would _____ our home value and _____ the extra

money to us. The _____ offered by the government will offset any debt for our future.

EXERCISE 3 Underline each word that is used incorrectly in the sentence. Then, in the blank, write the word that should have been used.

1. _____ I'm not reverse to helping you with your plan.

2. _____ Instead of going straight home, they took a circumvented route.

3. _____ The two countries made a bilingual agreement on arms limitation.

4. _____ We were fascinated as we watched the endomorphism of the pupa into a moth.

5. _____ In the botany lab, we detained a flower and named all its parts.

6. _____ We felt that the soprano gave too low an evaluation of our house.

7. _____ Averse road conditions made our trip unpleasant.

8. _____ The superpower tried to introvert the natives on the island.

9. _____ The secretary's proscription toward wasting time led to her dismissal.

10. _____ The bibliophile aided them after the famine.

11. _____ The rupture of the volcano required all the residents to be rescued.

12. _____ Suffering from claustrophobia, she refused to go to the top of the tower.

13. _____ I could not sustain from voting for the president of the United States in 2012.

14. _____ High schools require students who misbehave to take retention.

15. _____ His diabetes is due to an excess of hyperbole in his bloodstream.

EXERCISE 4 What name would you apply to a person:

1. Who denies the existence of God? _____

2. Who loves people and gives money to benefit them? _____

3. Who studies the development and behavior of human beings? _____

4. Who disagrees with the government? _____

5. Who gives the commencement address upon a graduation? _____

QUIZ YOURSELF   Visit the student companion website at www.cengagebrain.com to check your progress by working with the audio flashcards.

56   VERT, VERS—to turn

A **verse** or line of poetry comes from the root VERS *to turn*. Just as a plow makes a furrow and then at the end of the furrow *turns* to make another parallel one, so a verse of poetry *turns* when it comes to the end of the line and goes back to make another line.

Universe also comes from the root VERS. It is made up of UNI *one* and VERS *to turn* and means literally all things that exist *turned* into one. The ancients thought all the heavenly bodies were *turning* around the Earth, *turning* into one whole.

adversary (ad´ vur ser ē) [AD against + VERS to turn] noun—one turned against another; opponent. *She easily defeated her adversary in the tennis match.*

adversity (ad vur´ suh t ē) [AD against + VERS to turn] noun—the state of being turned against; misfortune. *The lawyer's early years of adversity made him sympathetic to others in trouble.*

averse (uh vurs´) [AB from + VERS to turn] adjective—to turn from; having a feeling of great distaste. *Having lost so much money on the lottery, she was averse to risking any more.*

aversion (uh vur´ zhun) [AB away + VERS to turn] noun—a turning away; extreme dislike. *Because of her aversion to work, my niece never held a job long.*

avert (uh vurt´) [AB away + VERT to turn] verb—to turn away. *She averted her eyes from the unpleasant scene.* Also, to prevent. *By taking preventive measures, they hope to avert another disaster.*

controversy (kahn´ truh vur s ē) [CONTRA against + VERS to turn] noun—opinions turned against each other; a dispute. *The controversy over the use of the land remained unsettled.*

convert (kun vurt´) [CON together + VERT to turn] verb—to turn together to the same belief; to turn from one belief to another. *They tried to convert me to their political beliefs.*

divert (duh vurt´) [DI away + VERT to turn] verb—to turn away, as to turn someone's attention away from something. *I tried to listen to the lecture, but the whispering behind me diverted my attention.*

extrovert (ex´ tro vurt) [EX out + VERT to turn] noun—one who turns outward; one whose thoughts and interests are directed outward; outgoing. *Warm and friendly, the extrovert enjoyed weekend parties.*

inadvertent (in ud vur tunt) [IN not + AD to + VERT to turn] adjective—not turning one's mind to a matter; unintentional. *Ian made an inadvertent reference to the plans for the surprise party.*

introvert (in´ truh vurt) [INTRO within + VERT to turn] noun—one who turns within; one whose thoughts and interests are directed inward. *Introverts prefer quiet evenings at home.*

perverse (pur vurs´) [PER (intensive) + VERS to turn] adjective—turned away from what is right or good; obstinately disobedient or difficult. *Always perverse, he opposed the wishes of the group.*

versatile (vur´ suh tul) adjective—able to turn easily from one subject or occupation to another; competent in many fields. *An unusually versatile actor, he is able to play any role from hero to clown.*

verse (vurs) [VERS to turn] noun—turning from one line to the next in poetry, like a plow turning to make parallel furrows. *I wrote an amusing new verse for my Christmas cards this year.*

vertebra (vur´ tuh bruh) noun—a bone of the spinal column that turns. *A vertebra is one of thirty-three short, thick bones through which the spinal cord runs.*

ALSO: anniversary, converse, conversion, diverse, diversify, diversion, divorce, incontrovertible, inverse, invertebrate, obverse, reverse, revert, subversive, version, versus (vs.), vertigo

✎ **EXERCISE 1**   **Write the appropriate VERT, VERS word.**

1. I'd rather have him as a partner than as a(n) _____ in the game.

2. I regretted having made a(n) _____ reference to her previous job.

3. Spending much time analyzing his thoughts, he was a true _____.

4. Completely disillusioned, he was _____ to giving any money to the project.

5. He faced the _____ with grace, which people admired.

6. During that year of _____, he lost his job and his home.

7. Our trip had to be postponed because of _____ weather.

8. When I stared at her, she _____ (ed) her eyes.

9. The child molester was sent to prison for his _____ actions.

10. Many early pagans _____ (ed) to Christianity during the Middle Ages.

11. Shakespeare is considered one of the best writers of poetic _____.

12. At the trial, the defendant's attorney tried to _____ the jurors' attention away from the facts by appealing to their emotions.

13. The _____ is easy to talk with, enjoying the company of others.

14. When I slipped on that banana peel, I bruised my _____.

15. Fred Astaire was a _____ performer; he could sing, dance, and act.

✎ **EXERCISE 2**   **As a review of some of the roots you have learned, make a root chain similar to the one on pages 1–3. Start with** *premise*, **and refer to the preceding pages to find the words you need.**

pre mise

pre cognitive

↓

pro gnosis

57 | VIA—way

In Roman times, a place where three roads met was called the three-*way* place, or **trivia** (TRI three + VIA way). When people on their way to market gathered at that place to chat about unimportant matters, their talk came to be called **trivia**, or three-*way* talk. Eventually any talk about unimportant things was called **trivial**. So today, when we talk about trivial things, we are reminded of those Romans who did likewise.

deviate (de´ ve āt) [DE from + VIA way] verb—to turn away from an established way. *Anyone who deviates from the rules is likely to be in trouble.*

deviation (de ve ā´ shun) [DE from + VIA way] noun—a turning aside from an established way. *The chairperson would not tolerate the slightest deviation from parliamentary rules.*

devious (de´ ve us) [DE from + VIA way] adjective—straying from the proper way; crooked. *His fortune had been made by devious means.*

impervious (im pur´ ve us) [IN not + PER through + VIA way] adjective—no way through; incapable of being passed through. *The cloth was impervious to water. His mind was impervious to reason.*

obviate (ob´ ve āt) [OB against + VIA way] verb—to meet and do away with something that is in the way; to do away with; to prevent. *Careful planning will obviate future difficulties.*

obvious (ob´ ve us) [OB against + VIA way] adjective—clearly visible; evident. *What we should do was obvious.*

previous (pre´ ve us) [PRE before + VIA way] adjective—under way beforehand. *I learned that in a previous assignment.*

trivia (triv´ e uh) [TRI three + VIA way] noun—any unimportant matters. *Knowledge of trivia is important for quiz show contestants.*

trivial (triv´ e ul) [TRI three + VIA way] adjective—unimportant. *Bruce became upset over the most trivial matters.*

via (vi´ uh) [VIA way] adjective—by way of. *We are going to Denver via Chicago.*

viaduct (vi´ uh dukt) [VIA way + DUC to lead] noun—a bridge leading a road (way) over a valley. *The viaduct takes the road over the railroad tracks.*

✎ **EXERCISE 1   Write the VIA word next to its definition.**

1. _____ by way of
2. _____ an unimportant matter
3. _____ to prevent
4. _____ straying from the proper way
5. _____ incapable of being passed through

✎ **EXERCISE 2   Write the appropriate VIA word.**

1. The Romans built the first bridges, called _____.
2. Plastic is a(n) _____ material.
3. Eating well may _____ the risk of heart disease.
4. Moral corruption leads to _____ behavior.
5. Some of my friends know lots of _____ and so can speak on almost any topic.
6. Do not _____ from the approved plan.
7. It is _____ that he is my good friend; he regularly empathizes with me.
8. Go north _____ the Great Road to get to the mall.
9. At the end of our meeting, we discussed _____ matters.
10. When drafting an essay, _____ from the premise will weaken your argument.

✎ **EXERCISE 3 JOURNAL   In your *vocabulary journal*, write four sentences using VERT and VIA words. Pick words that you have trouble remembering.**

58 VOC, VOKE—to call, voice

A **convocation** [CON together + VOC to call] is a *calling* together, an assembly. It may begin with an **invocation** [IN in + VOC to call], a *calling* for divine aid; and if the convocation is a college graduation, then the graduates will be looking forward to their **vocations**, or *callings*. Later, after they are settled in their jobs, they will no doubt be thinking of **avocations**, or *callings* away from their jobs.

advocate (ad´ vu kut) [AD to + VOC to call] noun—a person who pleads on another's behalf or for a cause. *The autocrat was not an advocate of free elections in his country.*

avocation (av u kā shun) [AB away + VOC to call] noun—a passion or a hobby. *My father spent his time on his avocation: building birdhouses.*

convocation (kahn vu kā´ shun) [CON together + VOC to call] noun—an assembly. *If I pass all of my courses this year, I will get my degree at the spring convocation.*

evoke (i vōk´) [E out + VOC to call] verb—to call forth, as memories or feelings. *The smell of burning leaves always evoke memories of his childhood.*

invocation (in vuh kā shun) [IN in + VOC to call] noun—an opening prayer. *The invocation was given by the guest rabbi.*

invoke (in vōk´) [IN in + VOC to call] verb—to call upon for aid or support. *The woman accused of larceny invoked the Fifth Amendment.*

irrevocable (i rev´ uh ku bul) [IN not + RE back + VOC to call] adjective—not capable of change; not alterable. *His decision was irrevocable; once the plan was executed it could not be brought back.*

provocation (prahv uh kā´ shun) [PRO forth + VOC to call] noun—something that is irritating or causes irritation. *That child cries at the slightest provocation.*

provoke (pruh vōk´) [PRO forth + VOC to call] verb—to cause anger or irritation. *His constant complaining provokes me.*

revoke (ri vōk´) [RE back + VOC to call] verb—to call back. *The company revoked its earlier offer.*

vocabulary (vō cab yO lar ē) noun—literally the words one can speak (call); the meaning of words. *A strong vocabulary is an asset in college.*

vocation (vo kā´ shun) noun—a calling; an occupation or a profession. *Are you pleased with your choice of vocation?*

vociferous (vō sif´ ur us) [VOC voice + FER to carry] adjective—carrying a loud voice; noisy. *The crowd at the rally made a vociferous protest against the location of the nuclear power plant.*

ALSO: advocacy, evocative, equivocal, equivocate, provocative, vocal

✎ **EXERCISE 1   Write the appropriate VOC, VOKE word.**

1. The chasm between the adversaries was _____.

2. Edna St. Vincent Millay's sonnets of love _____ strong pathos in the reader.

3. Inspirational leaders _____ their followers to be philanthropic and benevolent.

4. Although he liked his vocation, his _____ of guitar playing really satisfied him.

5. When the strikers marched in front of their building, they were _____ yet civil.

6. To obtain good grades in my nursing courses, I need a scientific _____.

7. Congress always begins its session with a(n) _____.

8. Awards were presented at the spring _____.

9. His license was _____ (ed) after his third conviction for DUI.

10. Marita found her _____ in teaching.

11. My school counselor is my _____.

12. Another dog's passing by is the _____ for my dog's howling.

13. Her nasty comments at the meeting _____ (ed) a stern reply from the dean.

✎ **EXERCISE 2 JOURNAL   In your *vocabulary journal*, write four sentences using VOC, VOKE words that give advice.**

EXERCISE 1 The twelve underlined words are ones you've studied. Copy them onto the lines below and give their meanings. Understanding all the words should make rereading the paragraph satisfying.

Faced in the 1980s with the <u>prospect</u> of <u>chronic</u> oil shortages, most Americans <u>concurred</u> that everyone must conserve. Government <u>edicts</u> reduced speed limits and controlled temperatures in public buildings. Individuals overcame their <u>propensity</u> to drive their cars to work and no longer regarded public transportation with <u>aversion</u>. Others experimented with a <u>spectrum</u> of solutions from windmills to solar power. All the efforts taken together, though not a <u>panacea</u> for our energy problems, were an important <u>prologue</u> to what we must do to make sure some oil supplies will be left for <u>posterity</u>. And still today, we are struggling to find ways to <u>circumvent</u> the <u>unprecedented</u> oil shortage that threatens us.

WORD	MEANING
1. _____	_____
2. _____	_____
3. _____	_____
4. _____	_____
5. _____	_____
6. _____	_____
7. _____	_____
8. _____	_____
9. _____	_____
10. _____	_____
11. _____	_____
12. _____	_____

EXERCISE 2 Underline the appropriate word.

1. A rabbit chasing a dog would be (preposterous, precipitous).

2. (Morpheus, Morphology) was the god of sleep.

3. Socrates was one of the early Western (philosophers, philodendrons) who we still study and revere.

4. To get her driver's license, she had to (verify, verity) her address.

5. A true (introvert, extrovert), he went out of his way to make friends.

6. I wasn't thinking when I made that (inadvertent, versatile) remark.

7. It is useful to write using (analogies, hyperboles) to show the relationship between conceptual ideas.

8. The (hologram, seismograph) accurately records the motion of the ground during an earthquake.

9. The (synergistic, syllogistic) work of everyone in the group really paid off.

10. (Assiduous, Insidious) workers often get their promotions faster than malingers and malcontents.

11. To most people, it is (cacophony, dissident), but I really enjoy the sounds of a (sympathy, symphony) orchestra tuning up.

12. She had learned to reason according to the classic (syllogisms, symphonies).

13. If you follow the rules, you'll (obviate, deviate) further trouble.

14. Her (perverse, reverse) attitude made her unpopular in the office.

15. His working full time may be an (impediment, expedient) to his success in college.

16. As they chatted about (trivia, viaduct) during the musical performance, they were (impervious, devious) to the glances of those around them.

17. As soon as the winner was announced, there was happy (pandemonium, xenophobia) in the stands.

18. Any (deviation, recession) in following the recipe may mean a ruined dinner.

19. In (retrospect, prospect), our decision to attend college was a good idea.

20. Walking home from the subway, we were caught in a (veritable, verifiable) downpour.

21. You may depend upon her to give a (veracious, tenacious) account of the proceedings.

22. Her husband was (detained, pertained) in Paris by business.

23. She tried to (divert, revert) the attention of her guests from her (perfidious, precocious) child.

24. My friends (refused, revived) to (speculate, specter) on the outcome of the election.

25. The (prologue, epilogue) was the perfect conclusion to the play.

26. In a (symbiotic, biofeedback) relationship, the shrimp digs a burrow for itself and the goby fish, and the goby fish warns the almost blind shrimp of danger by tapping the shrimp's tail.

QUIZ YOURSELF   Visit the student companion website at www.cengagebrain.com to check your progress by working with the audio flashcards.

COMPREHENSIVE TEST A

The words in this test are taken from the words you have learned throughout the book. Your score on this test will indicate how much the study of word roots has increased your vocabulary.

1. _____ **ambivalence** **A.** lack of feeling **B.** conflicting feelings **C.** good feeling **D.** no feeling

2. _____ **misanthropic** **A.** doubting **B.** hating marriage **C.** hating people **D.** generous

3. _____ **antithesis** **A.** secondary theme of an essay **B.** failure **C.** climax **D.** exact opposite

4. _____ **automaton** **A.** self-government **B.** government by a single person **C.** one who acts mechanically **D.** car buff

5. _____ **beneficiary** **A.** lawyer who handles wills **B.** one who receives benefits **C.** one who gives money to benefit others **D.** one who leaves money in a will

6. _____ **synchronize** **A.** to keep a time record **B.** to compose an accompaniment **C.** to cause to keep time together **D.** to prophesy

7. _____ **circumspect** **A.** cautious **B.** hardworking **C.** knowledgeable **D.** showing respect

8. _____ **compunction** **A.** connecting word **B.** compulsion **C.** satisfaction about something one has done **D.** a slight regret

9. _____ **incredulous** **A.** not believe readily **B.** believing too readily **C.** lacking credit **D.** not trustworthy

10. _____ **cursory** **A.** using profanity **B.** critical **C.** hateful **D.** hasty and superficial

11. _____ **demagogue** **A.** ancient tribal god **B.** half man and half god **C.** leader who appeals to the emotions of the people to gain power **D.** leader who works for the good of the people

12. _____ **euphonious** **A.** having a pleasant sound **B.** coming from a distance **C.** false **D.** difficult to hear

13. _____ **exonerate** **A.** to honor **B.** to take out objectionable parts **C.** to free from blame **D.** to find guilty

14. _____ **eulogy** **A.** speech by an actor alone on the stage **B.** explanation of a literary passage **C.** speech blaming someone **D.** speech praising someone

15. _____ **colloquial** **A.** incorrect **B.** talkative **C.** informal conversation **D.** standard

16. _____ **malevolent** **A.** kindly **B.** violent **C.** giving money to others **D.** wishing evil toward others

17. _____ **premise** **A.** traveler **B.** initial statement assumed to be true **C.** servant **D.** a stopping and starting at intervals

18. _____ **metamorphosis** **A.** relating to the early Stone Age **B.** resembling humans **C.** having animal form **D.** changing form

19. _____ **panoply** **A.** impressive display **B.** high covering **C.** harsh criticism **D.** series of games

20. _____ **apathetic**   A. sad   B. deserving sympathy   C. pitiful   D. indifferent

21. _____ **expedite**   A. to experiment with   B. to send away   C. to speed the progress of   D. to make clear

22. _____ **propensity**   A. dislike   B. thoughtfulness   C. belief   D. natural inclination

23. _____ **sedentary**   A. temporary   B. permanent   C. requiring much sitting   D. producing sediment

24. _____ **specious**   A. having many rooms   B. seemingly good but actually not so   C. reasonable   D. category of living things

25. _____ **subterfuge**   A. deceptive strategy   B. underwater vessel   C. play acting   D. hatred

26. _____ **insuperable**   A. extraordinary   B. easily overcome   C. incapable of being overcome   D. best of its kind

27. _____ **symbiosis**   A. similarity in biologic function   B. similarity in evolutionary development   C. living together for mutual benefits of survival   D. use of symbols in literature

28. _____ **bicameral**   A. two marriages   B. two branches of government   C. two sides   D. two teams

29. _____ **philodendron**   A. a stamp collector   B. a tropical climbing plant   C. one who loves books   D. one who loves people

30. _____ **bankrupt**   A. having more power or importance   B. judgment formed beforehand   C. a preference for something   D. unable to pay outstanding debts

31. _____ **synergy**   A. the way words are arranged   B. a brief general summary   C. working together   D. type of illness

32. _____ **obviate**   A. to turn away from an established way   B. no way through   C. to do away with or prevent   D. evident

33. _____ **vociferous**   A. loud, noisy voice   B. to call back   C. talkative   D. unalterable

34. _____ **avert**   A. lines of poetry   B. to turn inside   C. to turn away   D. unfavorable

35. _____ **tortuous**   A. inflicting physical or mental pain   B. to annoy   C. full of twists and turns   D. a turtle

36. _____ **prognosticate**   A. to put off doing something   B. forecast or prediction   C. pouring forth freely   D. awareness of the thinking process

37. _____ **abstain**   A. to mean harm   B. to stick together   C. to feel good   D. to refrain deliberately

38. _____ **hyperbole**   A. overreaching   B. farsightedness   C. a figure of speech that uses exaggeration   D. large stomach that protrudes

39. _____ **anarchy**   A. political disorder and confusion   B. without caring   C. one who does not believe in God   D. not typical

40. _____ **monologue**   A. speech before a play   B. the king or ruler   C. speech by one person   D. a hymn to God

COMPREHENSIVE TEST B

These words contain all the roots you have studied. Give the meaning of each root and the meaning of the word.

WORD	ROOT	MEANING OF ROOT	MEANING OF WORD
1. ambivalent	AMBI	_____	_____
2. antedate	ANTE	_____	_____
3. anthropomorphism	ANTHROP	_____	_____
	MORPH	_____	
4. antibiotic	ANTI	_____	_____
	BIO	_____	
5. asymmetric	A	_____	_____
	SYM	_____	
	METR	_____	
6. seismograph	GRAPH	_____	_____
7. benediction	BENE	_____	_____
	DICT	_____	
8. biennial	BI	_____	_____
	ENN	_____	
9. chronometer	CHRON	_____	_____
	METER	_____	
10. circumscribe	CIRCUM	_____	_____
	SCRIB	_____	
11. colloquial	COL	_____	_____
	LOQU	_____	
12. convert	CON	_____	_____
	VERT	_____	
13. credible	CRED	_____	_____

WORD	ROOT	MEANING OF ROOT	MEANING OF WORD
14. erupt	E	_____	_____
	RUPT	_____	
15. equate	EQU	_____	_____
16. euphony	EU	_____	_____
	PHON	_____	
17. evoke	E	_____	_____
	VOC	_____	
18. expedient	EX	_____	_____
	PED	_____	
19. fidelity	FID	_____	_____
20. genealogy	GEN	_____	_____
	-LOGY	_____	
21. malady	MAL	_____	_____
22. monosyllable	MONO	_____	_____
	SYL	_____	
23. pandemic	PAN	_____	_____
	DEM	_____	
24. philanthropy	PHIL	_____	_____
	ANTHROP	_____	
25. tenacious	TEN	_____	_____
26. prologue	PRO	_____	_____
	LOG	_____	
27. prospectus	PRO	_____	_____
	SPECT	_____	

28. retain   RE   _____   _____

                      TAIN   _____

29. subside   SUB   _____   _____

                      SID   _____

30. superannuated   SUPER   _____   _____

                      ANN   _____

31. apathetic   A   _____   _____

                      PATH   _____

32. prognosis   PRO   _____   _____

                      GNOS   _____

33. verify   VER   _____   _____

34. amorphous   A   _____   _____

                      MORPH   _____

35. precede   PRE   _____   _____

                      CEDE   _____

36. panacea   PAN   _____   _____

37. cursory   CUR   _____

38. hypercritical   HYPER   _____   _____

39. vociferous   VOC, VOKE   _____   _____

40. posthumously   POST   _____   _____

COMPREHENSIVE TEST C

Here are all 58 roots that you have learned. Give the meaning of each root and a word in which it is found.

ROOT	MEANING	WORD
1. A, AN		
2. AMBI, AMPHI		
3. ANN, ENN		
4. ANTE, ANTI		
5. ANTHROP		
6. ANTI		
7. AUTO		
8. BENE		
9. BI		
10. BIO		
11. CEDE, CEED		
12. CHRON		
13. CIRCUM		
14. COGNI, GNOS		
15. COM, CON, COL, COR		
16. CRED		
17. CUR		
18. DEM		
19. DICT		
20. DIS, DI, DIF		
21. EQU		
22. EU		
23. EX, ES, E		
24. FID		
25. GEN		
26. GRAPH, GRAM		
27. HYPER		

ROOT	MEANING	WORD
28. LOG		
29. -LOGY		
30. LOQU, LOC		
31. MAL		
32. METER, METR		
33. MIT, MIS, MISS		
34. MONO		
35. MORPH		
36. PAN		
37. PATH		
38. PED		
39. PHIL		
40. PHOB		
41. PHON		
42. POST		
43. PRE		
44. PRO		
45. RE		
46. RUPT		
47. SCRIB, SCRIPT		
48. SED, SID, SESS		
49. SPEC, SPIC, SPECT		
50. SUB		
51. SUPER		
52. SYN, SYM, SYL		
53. TAIN, TEN, TIN		
54. TORT		
55. VER		
56. VERT, VERS		
57. VIA		
58. VOC, VOKE		

COMPREHENSIVE TEST D

Underline the appropriate word in each sentence.

1. Many people think there should be a law permitting (euthanasia, monks).
2. Understanding a (symphony, cacophony) or a school of painting is just as much a (cognitive, corrupt) act as learning to read and write.
3. Her towels were embroidered with her (monogram, cardiogram).
4. The new plastic heart in his body ticked like a (metronome, meter).
5. "All leaves are green" is a false (premise, demise).
6. They studied a map showing the (calligraphy, topography) of the area they were entering.
7. A(n) (hyperbole, epigram) is a short, witty saying.
8. The governor was (diffident, confidant) in his debate with his opponent.
9. (Intermittent, Omitted) showers in Hawaii are called "liquid sunshine."
10. The review board (exonerated, excoriated) him, and he (retained, detained) his job.
11. She felt no (malice, malaise) toward the person who had been hired to replace her.
12. He had recently been diagnosed with a (congenial, genetic) (malady, maladroit).
13. A (genial, generic) clerk took time to explain why my steam iron had malfunctioned.
14. The job he was given was not (commensurate, commodious) with his ability.
15. Her (hyperglycemia, hyperbaton) is treated with medicine, exercise, and diet.
16. The physician identified the (malignant, malingerer) tumor by examining the (pathology, anthropology) of the cells.
17. He felt (apathetic, assiduous), not caring about his job.
18. The (ante meridiem, anterior) legs of an animal are those at the front.
19. The new highway (bicuspid, bisects) the city.
20. A (coherent, commodious) paper is well organized and sticks to the point.

COMPREHENSIVE TEST E

Underline each word that you have recently learned, and then give the meaning of the word. Many sentences use more than one word you have studied.

1. Punctuating a sentence incorrectly can distort its meaning. _____

2. Her kitchen contained a full panoply of modern and colorful equipment. _____, _____

3. The speaker was eloquent in his speech even though he was loquacious. _____, _____

4. His unpleasant retort may precipitate a quarrel. _____, _____

5. Her road to fame had been tortuous, with many wins and many losses. _____

6. Eating well and exercise can presage good health. _____

7. We had fun wandering through that subterranean cave with our headlamps. _____

8. The captors tried to extort a confession from their captive. _____

9. The endomorph has a protuberant belly even though he runs five miles every day. _____, _____

10. Some syndromes cannot be cured; agoraphobia and claustrophobia are two examples. _____, _____, _____

11. Anyone with a sedentary job needs to get plenty of exercise. _____

12. Franz Kafka wrote the tale of Gregor Samsa in the novel, *The Metamorphosis*, the tale of a man becoming an insect. _____

13. The doctor was unusually perspicacious in diagnosing the illness. _____, _____

14. The child was precocious but had a preponderance of emotional problems. _____, _____

15. The ads flashing on the screen for milliseconds had a subliminal effect on the viewers. _____

16. Their report was a synthesis of the ideas that had been presented at the symposium. _____, _____

17. The film director was given profuse praise by the grateful cast. _____

18. The postmortem was performed on the murdered suspect in the Sherlock Holmes' TV show, *Elementary*. _____

19. A four-year-old is amazingly credulous and will believe anything you say. _____

20. Receiving that scholarship expedited my getting through college. _____

Word Index